AF261457

ROCOCO

Author: Klaus H. Carl and Victoria Charles

Layout:
Baseline Co. Ltd,
District 3, Ho Chi Minh City
Vietnam

ISBN: 978-1-68325-934-3

Printed in

Klaus H. Carl & Victoria Charles

ROCOCO

Grace, intimacy, and the art of pleasure in 18th century

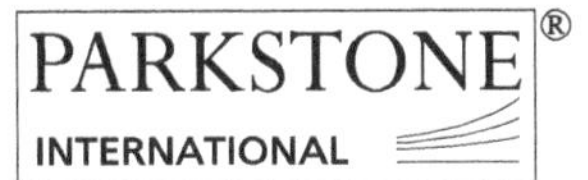

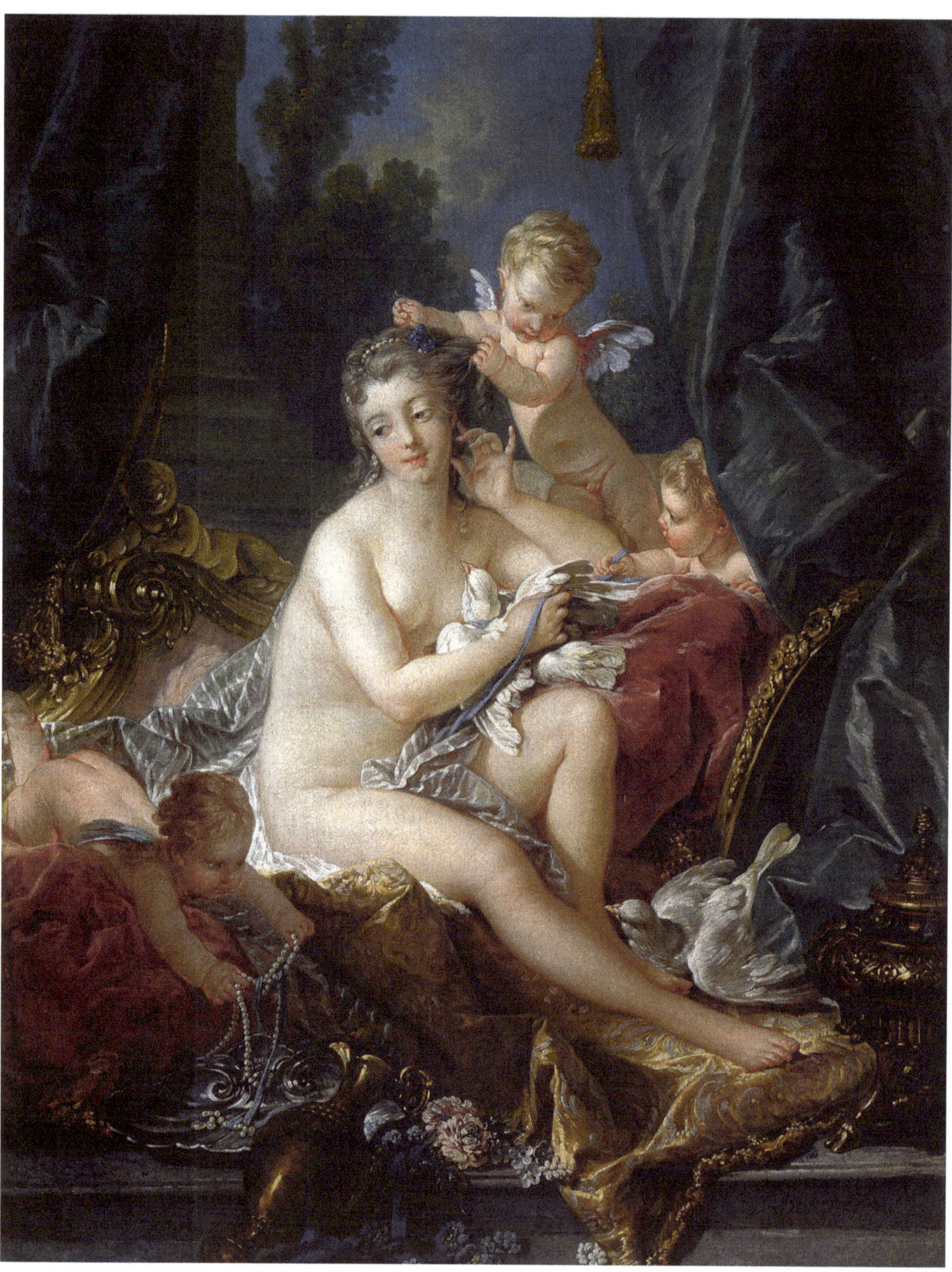

CONTENTS

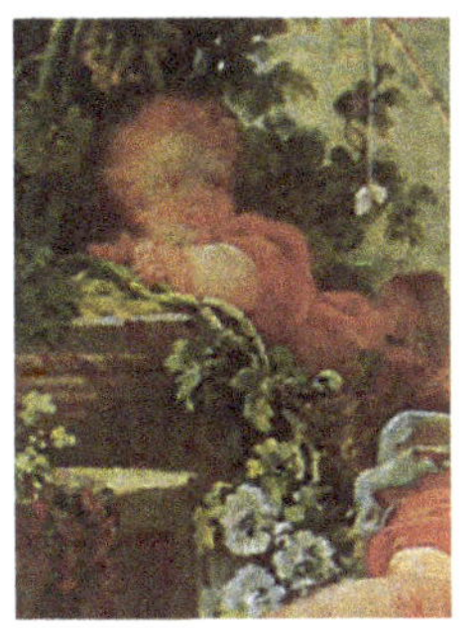

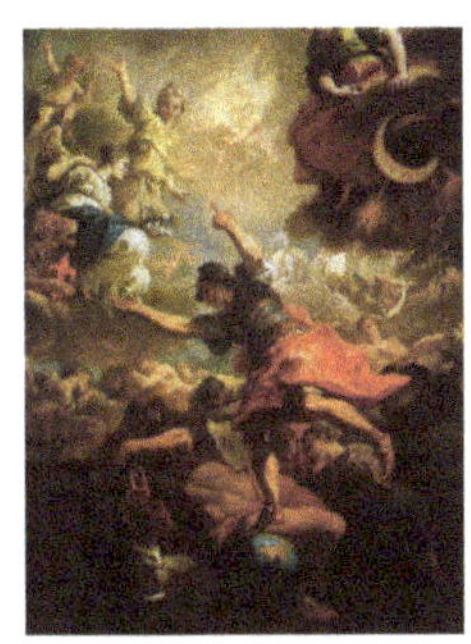

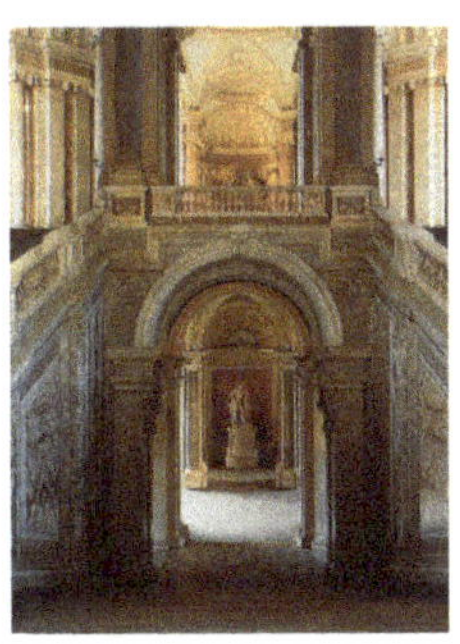

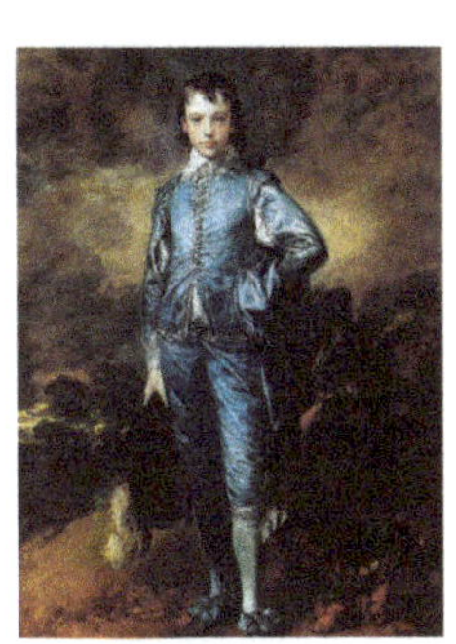

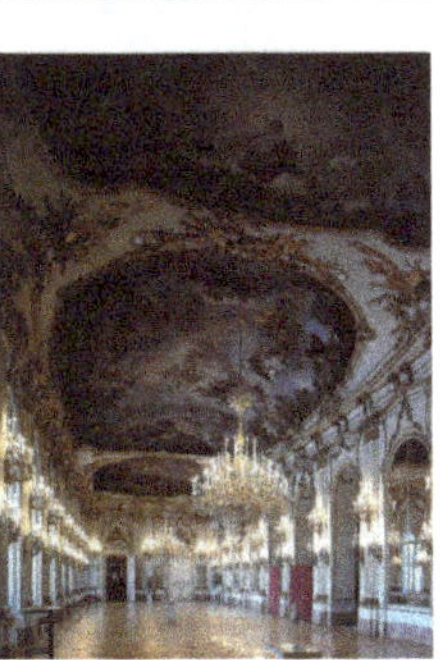

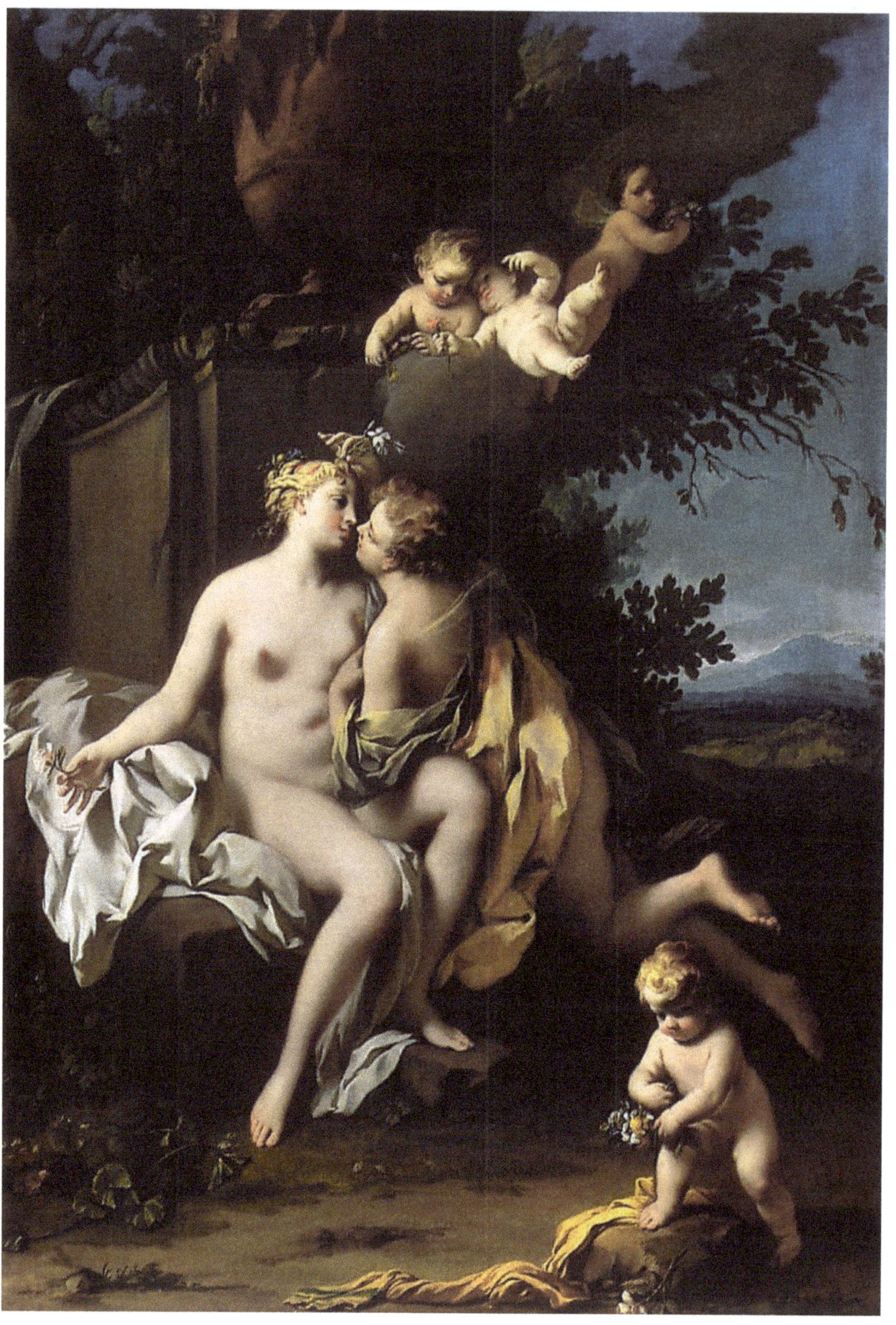

INTRODUCTION

n the first quarter of the 18th century, in a barely noticeable transition, Baroque gave way to Rococo, also known as the late Baroque period. The unstoppable victory parade of the Age of Enlightenment, which began with the Renaissance and the Reformation continued its unwavering march until the end of the 17th century in England, inching inexorably towards its climax, and throughout the 17th century formed the intellectual and cultural life of the entire 18th century. With this, the educated and prosperous bourgeoisie began to discuss works of art which had hitherto been largely left up to the nobility and the royal courts. If up until that point the clientele for architecture or paintings was drawn predominantly from the church and to a lesser extent from the nobility, and the artists were regarded rather as artisans organized into guilds, they now became individuals with independent professions. At the same time the artist was no longer obligated to create portraits or works based on mythology in accordance with never-changing, prescribed themes and commissions.

The most important instrument of the Enlightenment was prose, which was given a witty, inspirational, entertaining and universally comprehensible form in letters, pamphlets, treatises and historical works, since only these were able to reach the broad mass of the population. In France, between 1751 and 1775, the 29 volumes of the *Encyclopédie* were published jointly by Denis Diderot, Jean-Jacques Rousseau, d'Alembert and Voltaire. This encyclopaedia encompassed not only the whole of human knowledge but also made available a collection of arguments against the fossilisation of learning.

Absolutism was the norm, in an era in which rulers possessed unbridled power over their territories and were able to govern without any external controls or any obligation to their subjects. This era ended in France around the time of the death of Louis XIV (1715).

▲ **François Boucher,**
The Toilet of Venus, 1751.
Oil on canvas, 108.3 x 85.1 cm.
The Metropolitan Museum of Art, New York.

◀ **Jacopo Amigoni,**
Flora and Zephyr, 1748.
Oil on canvas, 213.4 x 147.3 cm.
The Metropolitan Museum of Art, New York

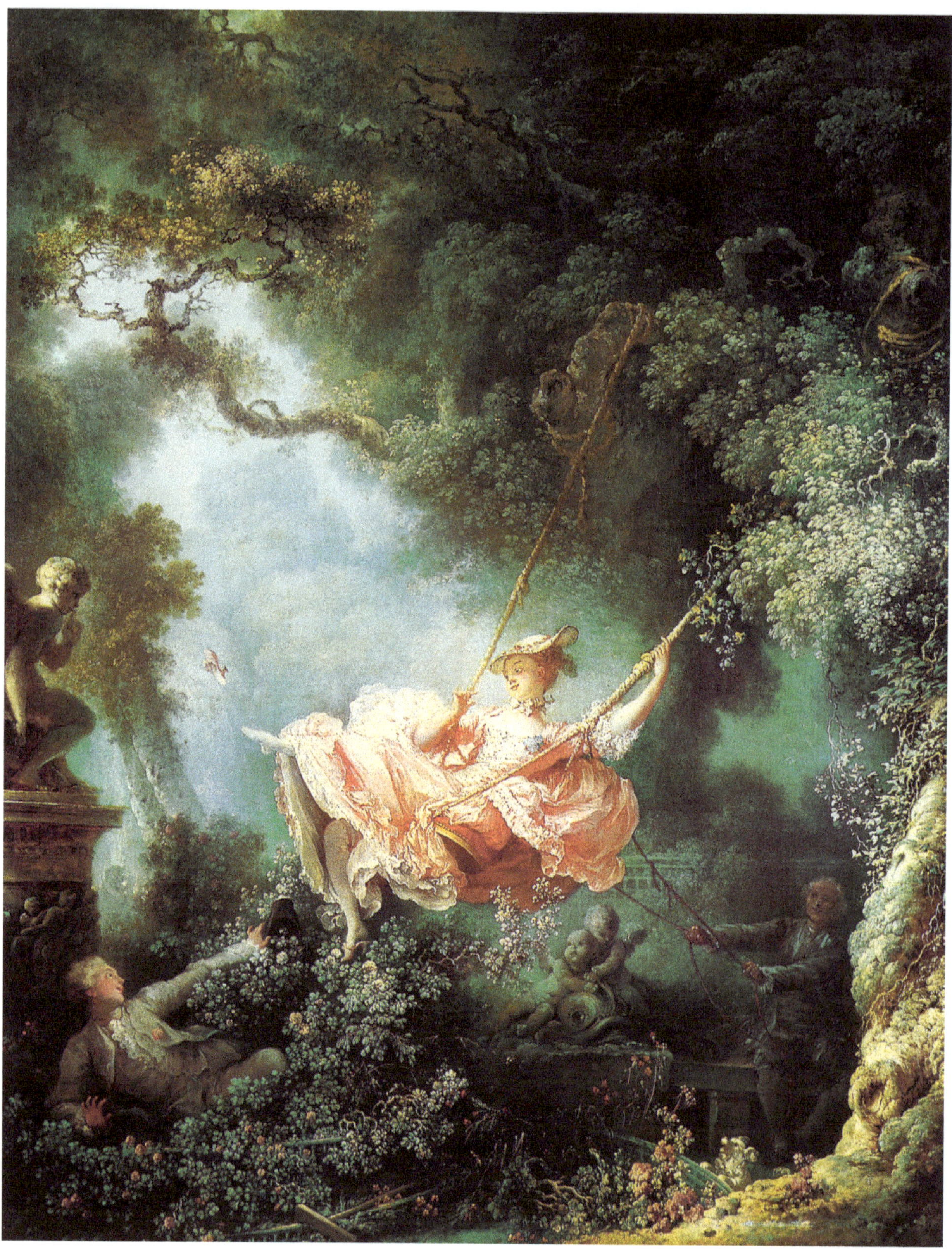

The Rococo In France

The man who should seek by personal observation of existing works of art to enter into the spirit of the Rococo must travel far indeed: for Paris, though the cradle of that vivacious style contains but fragments of the ancient glory. For precious examples of a noble conception of space he must seek in Versailles and Fontainebleau, for the greatest treasures of artistic French metal work in Nancy, and for remnants of exquisite silver as far as Lisbon or Petersburg – if, indeed, they have survived these troublous times. That unity of exterior and interior, of architecture and decoration, the full harmony of all that Rococo stood for, he can light upon only by travelling eastward across the frontiers of France and visiting the luxurious palaces of princes of Church and State in Germany; for example, Brühl, Bruchsal, Ansbach, Würzburg, Munich and Potsdam. And, finally, for a thorough acquaintance with the furniture of the period he must cross the Channel to the home of Chippendale and his associates.

◀ **Jean-Honoré Fragonard**,
The Swing, 1767.
Oil on canvas, 81 x 64.2 cm.
The Wallace Collection, London.

When Louis XIV died, the field in France was open, and the Rubensists took the lead, bringing forth a style we call Rococo, which – roughly translated – means 'pebblework Baroque', a decorative version of painterly Baroque. Rather than a continuation of the style of Rubens, the manner of Antoine Watteau, Jean-Honoré Fragonard and François Boucher conveyed a lighter mood, with more feathery strokes of the brush, a lighter palette and even a smaller size of canvas. Erotic subject matter and light genre subjects came to dominate the style, which found favour especially among the pleasure-loving aristocrats of France, as well as their peers elsewhere in continental Europe.

Rococo painters thus carried forward the debate between line and colour that had emerged in practice and theory in the sixteenth century. The argument between Michelangelo and Titian, and then between Rubens and Poussin, was a struggle that would not go away, and would return in the nineteenth century and later. Not every artist succumbed to Rococo. A focus in the eighteenth century on particular social virtues – patriotism, moderation, duty to the family, the necessity to embrace reason and study the laws of nature – were themselves at odds with the subject matter naturalism that reflected the spirit of the age. A number of artists, such as Elisabeth Vigée-Lebrun and Thomas Gainsborough, incorporated into their paintings some of the lightness of touch that characterised the Rococo, but they modified its excesses and avoided some of its artificial and superficial qualities, however delightful these are.

A leitmotif of Western painting has been the persistence of classicism, and here the Rococo found its fiercest opponent. The essentials of the classical style – a dynamic equilibrium, idealised naturalism, measured harmony, restraint of colour and a dominance of line, all operating under the guiding influence of ancient Greek and Roman models – reasserted themselves in the late-eighteenth century in response to Rococo. When Jacques-Louis David exhibited his *Oath of the Horatii* in 1785, it electrified the public, and was applauded by the French including the king, gaining an international audience. Thomas Jefferson happened to be in Paris at the time of the painting's exhibition and was greatly impressed. The popularity of Neoclassicism preceded the French Revolution, but once the revolution occurred, it became the official style of the virtuous new French regime. Rococo was associated with the decadent *ancien* régime, whose painters were forced to flee the country or change their styles.

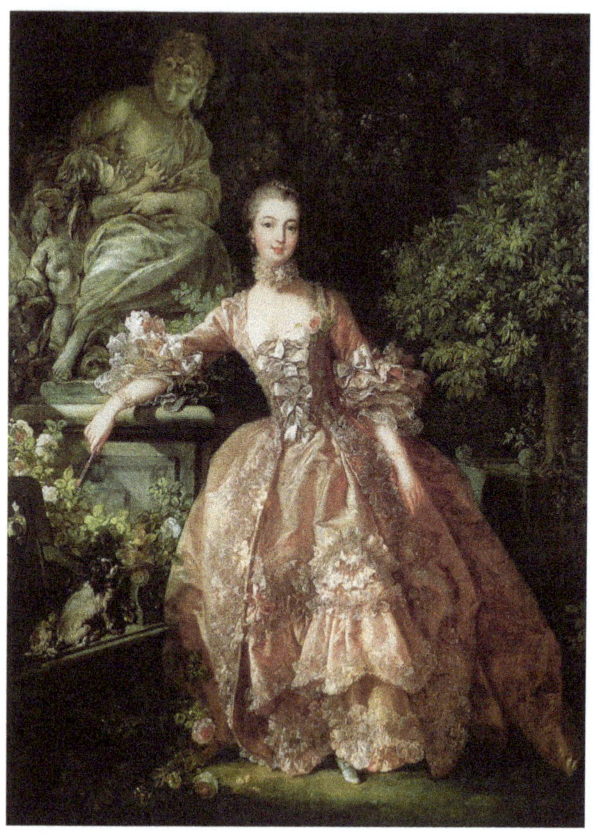

▲ **François Boucher,**
Madame de Pompadour, 1759.
Oil on canvas, 91 x 68 cm.
The Wallace Collection, London.

and hedonistic style of Rococo painters. In the realm of art theory and criticism, the philosophers and writers Diderot and Voltaire were unhappy with the Rococo style flourishing in France, and its days were numbered. The humble naturalism of the French artist Chardin was based in the Dutch still-life artistry of the previous century, while Anglo-American and English painters such as John Singleton Copley of Boston, Joseph Wright of Derby and Thomas Hogarth painted in styles which, in different ways, embodied a kind of fundamental

Jean-Honoré Fragonard, ▶
Blind-Man's Bluff, c. 1750-1752.
Oil on canvas, 114 x 90 cm.
Toledo Museum of Art, Toledo (Ohio).

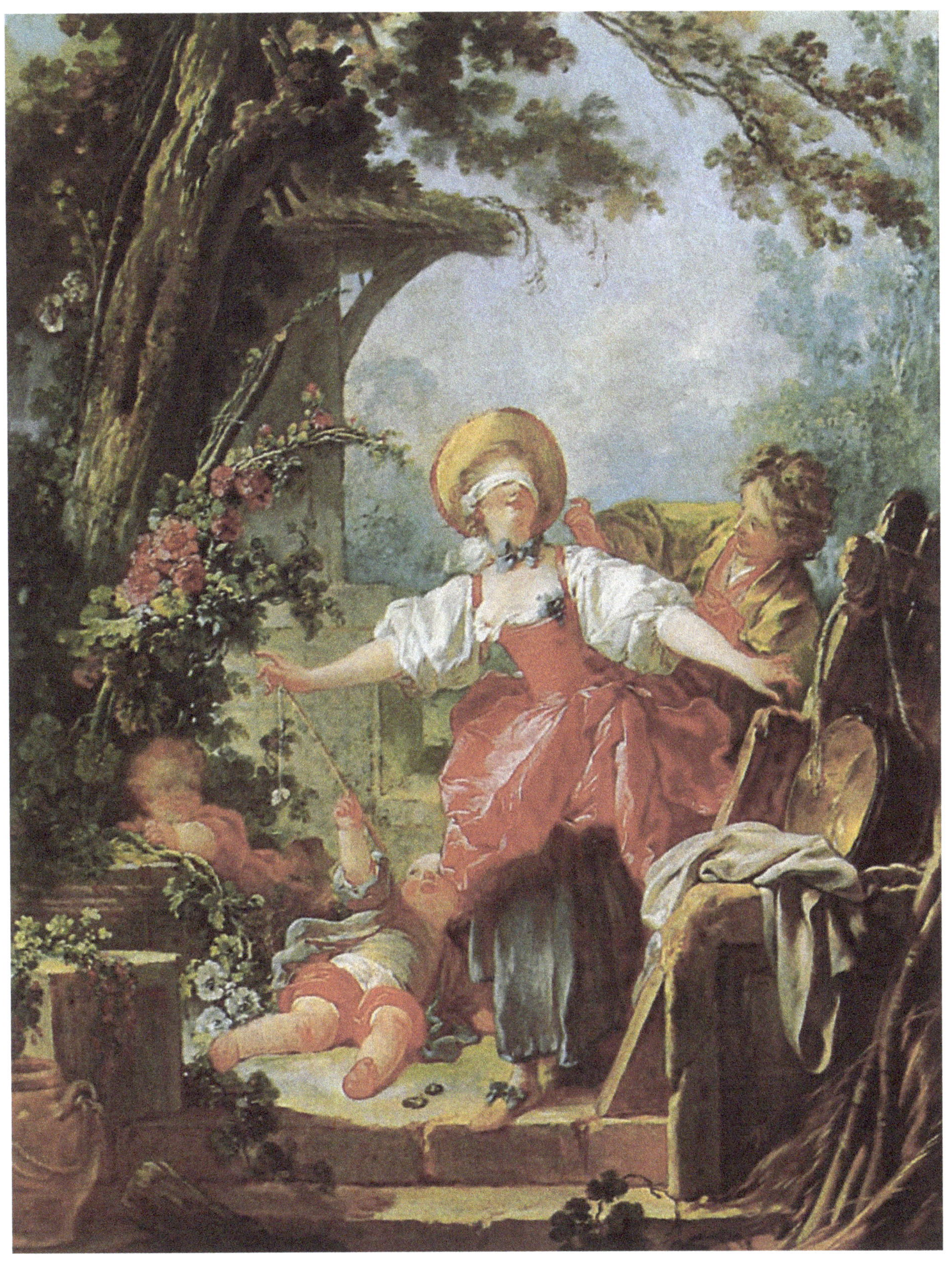

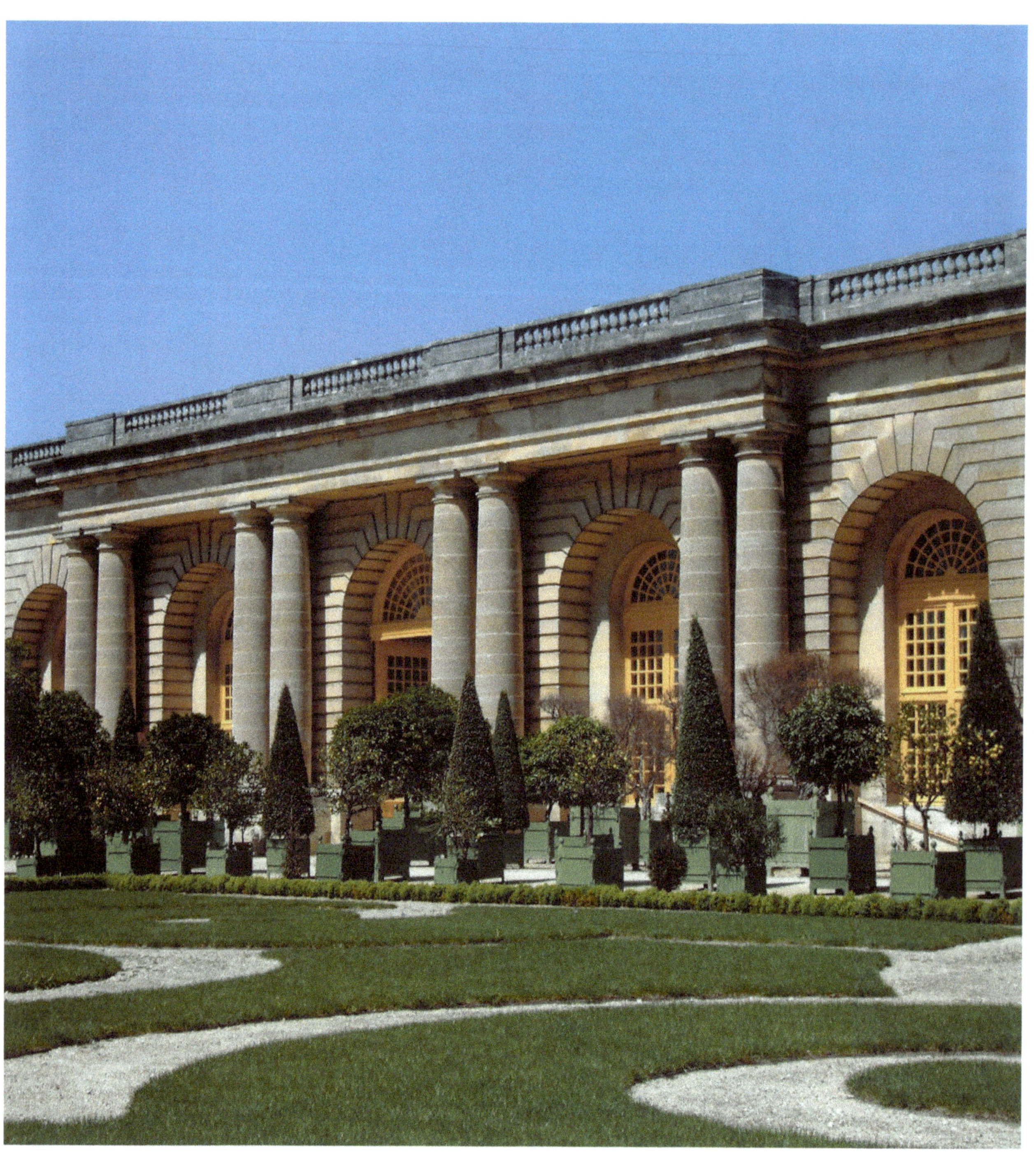

Architecture

Architecture adapted quite easily to the new trends in taste. Even at the beginning of the 17th century some theoreticians, probably under the influence of the Italian architecture critic Andrea Palladio, had demanded greater simplicity, greater symmetry and a distinctly quieter language of form. Strict classicism asserted itself in the external structure throughout the 18th century, although, in the meantime, shortly after the death of Louis XIV and under the Regency of Philip II of Orleans, the Rococo style – consequently also called by the French the "Style Régence" – had emerged. Of course this new style was restricted almost exclusively to interior decoration and the arts and crafts, which was responsible for its more elegant furniture, accessories and wall-coverings. The ponderous ostentation of the Baroque ornamentation in sculptural embellishment and in its colourful appearance was made lighter and brighter, and any remaining straight line dissolved into sweeping scrolls.

◀ **Jules Hardouin-Mansart,**
Orangerie, 1684-1686.
Domaine national du château de Versailles,
Versailles

By a carefully considered, well-planned division of the rooms, by each space's connection with the others and by the ubiquitous ornamentation, the decorative style of the mouldings became distinctive. The corners of the mouldings were broken and curved. Into the spaces that this created, little ornaments or flowers were then inserted, and later the mouldings, too, were wrapped with leaves and flowers and the straight lines were transformed into curved lines. Alongside the flirtatious curves and dainty arcs, beside the constantly increasing revitalisation of the floral and tendril-shaped ornaments, the intentional avoidance of rigid symmetry was one of the most striking symbols of Rococo decoration.

Amongst the most famous decorative artists are Juste-Aurèle Meissonnier, Gilles-Marie Oppenord and François de Cuvilliés, who had also been active in Munich. Their powers of invention and the richness of their imagination can be seen through their engravings and drawings. It also becomes clear here that Italian grotesque was the basis of French ornamentation. The ornamental artists also exerted a considerable influence on the other ornamentation of public buildings, particularly on the blacksmith's work on balustrades, banisters and wrought iron gates.

In French architecture in the 17th century, there was a counter-movement against the pompous, heavy Baroque style of Charles Le Brun, with a strict classicism that predominated in the extension of the Louvre by Claude Perrault. His main works as an architect are the eastern and southern external façades of the Louvre. However, an original French style of building was created only by the leading architect of the age, Jules Hardouin-Mansart, who at the young age of 30 was named Court Architect to his sovereign and invented the most effective decorative forms of the Baroque style with the structural rigidity of classicism.

The sphere of his major work was in fact the Palace of Versailles with its chapel, royal chambers, the Grand Trianon the Orangerie, built for the last mistress of Louis XIV, the Marquise de Maintenon. The most important of his artistic works is the dome of Les Invalides completed in 1708, the cupola of which is a masterly combination of monumental effect and French elegance. Hardouin-Mansart, in all of his works, created the foundations for the elegant decorative lines of the architecture and the ornamentation of the façades.

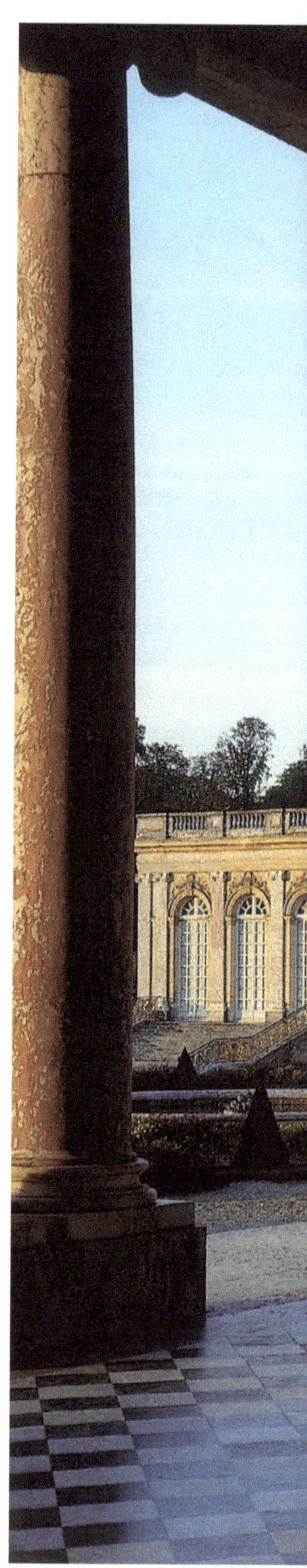

Jules Hardouin-Mansart, ▶
Grand Trianon, 1787-1788.
Domaine national du château de Versailles,
Versailles.

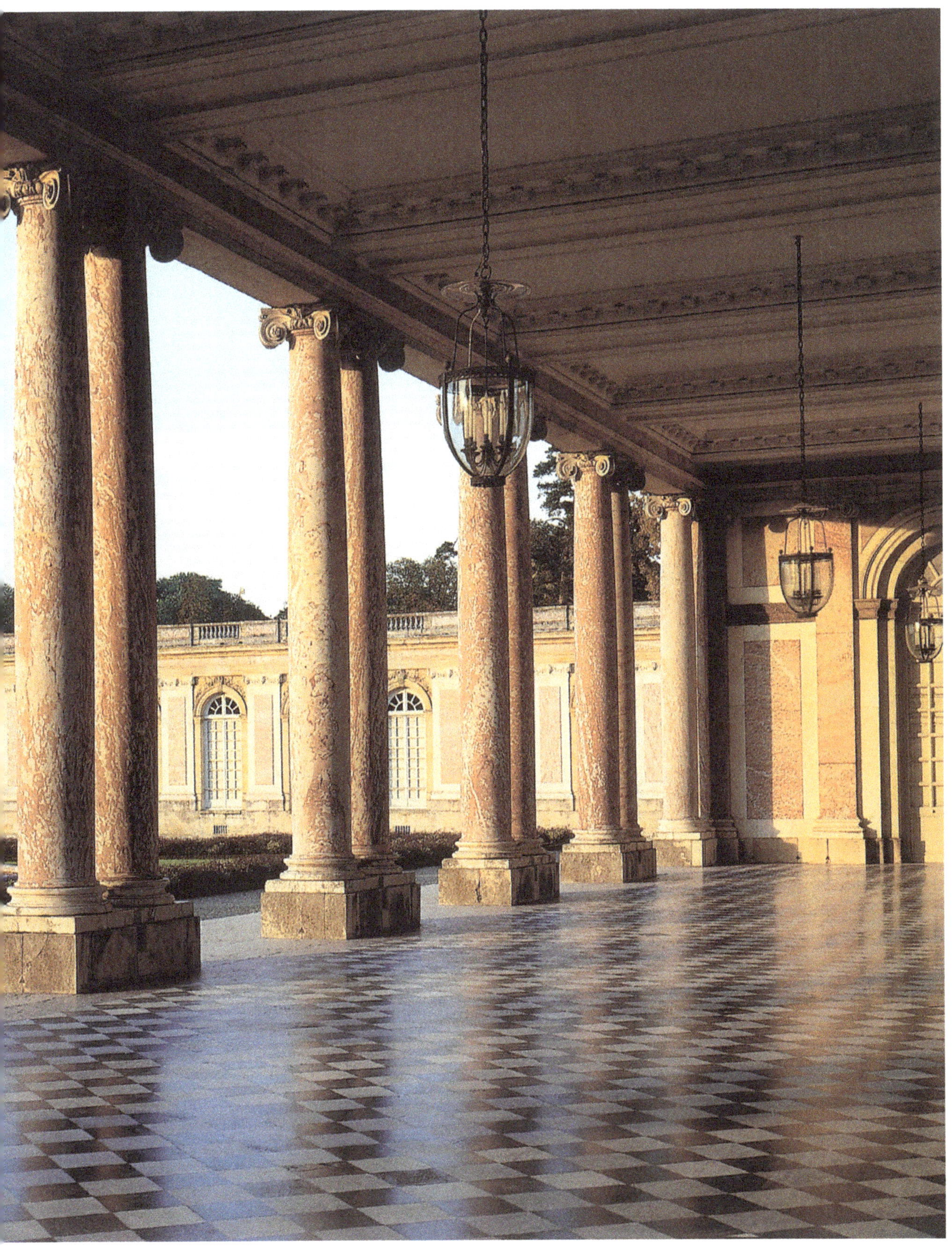

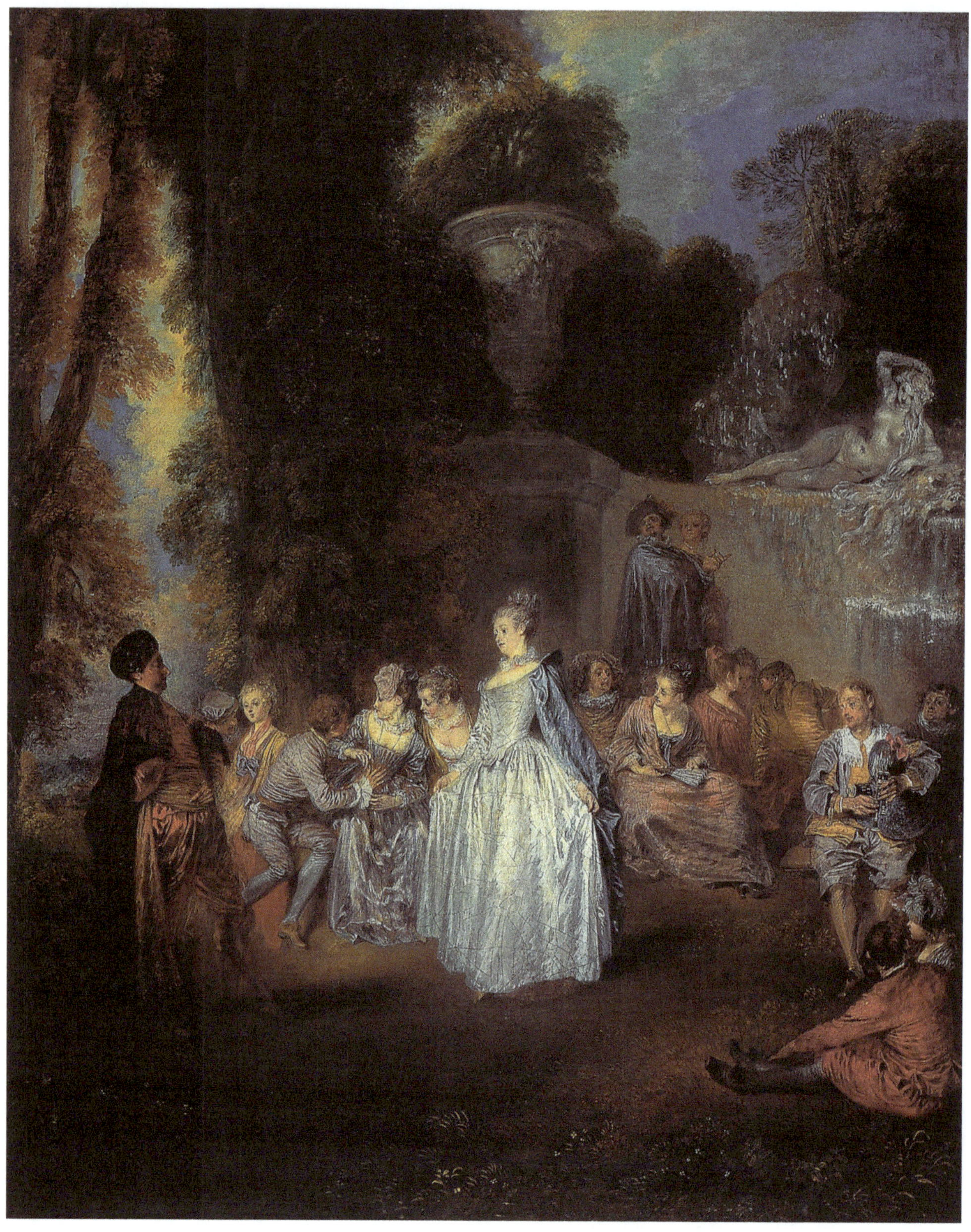

Painting

In the 18th century, the cold representation of the pictures of 17th-century designs gradually began to give way to a warmer conception, which developed further and further, manifesting itself ultimately in a frivolity of expression. French art in the 18th century finally discovered its own language. As painting with oils was an extensive process, Pastel painting, which developed as early as the Renaissance, became a fashionable medium, in particular for portrait painting. Pastel painting had been used earlier by Leonardo da Vinci, Hans Holbein the Younger and others, but with far less wealth of colour nuance than that which was displayed by the Rococo painters.

Antoine Watteau (1684-1721) was one of the key figures in Rococo art. Of Flemish origin, he came to Paris around 1702, where his interest in genre painting and in the world of theatre was aroused. Through the influence of Rubens, his style did not change so much as his subject matter – the "gay, wanton party". After the pomp of Louis XIV, artists

now concentrated on the pleasant, the private and the delicate. In the political sphere and aesthetic movements, there was a noticeable relaxation – art reacted to it with intimate, decorative and erotic motifs and mythological scenes. The pleasures of the flesh celebrated in his pastoral pieces were perhaps really a glorification of true love – at any rate, they portrayed the most hedonistic joys of life. Watteau possessed the rare gift of atmospheric colouration, which even in the brightest light still conveyed gentleness, mystery and a kind of musicality, combined with great artistic skill which put him on a par with the masters.

Watteau was the most brilliantly sophisticated painter of the 18th century who, despite his short life, dogged by problems of constant ill health, nevertheless created a series of masterpieces which have never lost their effectiveness that transcended the taste of the age. Watteau derived the Rococo style from the decorative style of the age of Louis XIV, in association with Chinese and Japanese forms of ornamentation characterised by the decorative painting in rooms, boudoirs and salons.

Amongst Watteau's best works are *The Lesson in Love* (c. 1716), *The Pilgrimage to the Island of*

◀ **Antoine Watteau**,
Fêtes Vénitiennes, 1718-1719.
Oil on canvas, 55.9 x 45.7 cm.
National Gallery of Scotland, Edinburgh.

Cythera and *The Dance* (between 1710 and 1720). The *Gersaint's Shop Sign* (1720), a sign painted for the Paris art dealer Gersaint, depicted the interior of the sale room and the distinguished visitors, thus capturing the reality of the time. One of his most beautiful pictures, *The Surprise* (c. 1718), had been missing since the mid-19th century and presumed to be destroyed until 2008, when it was discovered in an English country house and soon afterwards sold at auction for more than €15 million.

François Boucher (1903-1770) was the favourite artist of Louis XV and his mistress, Madame de Pompadour. Boucher wanted to please his contemporaries by embellishing their walls and ceilings and in this sense he embodied the taste of the century more than anyone else; he had a gift for composition, which he always expressed with a light touch, elegance and perfect harmony. As early as 1723, Boucher won the much sought-after Prix de Rome, which included a four-year stay in Rome. He was incredibly productive, creating mythological scenes with seductive goddesses, for example *Diana after Bathing* (1742), and pastoral scenes with alluring activities. In addition, he illustrated books and created designs for tapestries, models for porcelain figures, as well as fans and theatre decorations.

As a decorative artist he was by no means inferior to his fascinating Italian contemporary Tiepolo . In addition he painted outstanding portraits, for example the two portraits of Madame de Pompadour of 1750 and 1759, as well as intimate domestic scenes such as the *Morning Coffee* or *The Milliner* (1746). As a painter of portraits, Boucher was always pleasing and flattering, and as a chivalrous phrasemonger, he created a world which was far removed from reality, buried under a thick layer of powder and makeup, as in his *Venus in Vulcan's Smithy* (1757). After the French Revolution, Boucher disappeared almost completely and was not rediscovered until the end of the 19th century.

Jean-Honoré Fragonard (1732-1806), one of Boucher's best and most talented students, was the son of a perfume manufacturer. He came from Grasse, the city of perfume. He essentially painted romantic gardens with fountains, grottoes, temples and terraces and continued this chivalrous and successful tradition, for instance with *The Bathers* (1756), with the famous *The Swing* and *The Stolen Kiss*. The storms of revolution brought a violent end to this kind of art.

Jean-Siméon Chardin (1699-1779) was one of the most important colourists of the 18th century. Originally a still-life painter, he had then extended his work to the depiction of objects from daily life, as in *Cook Cleaning Turnips* (1738). These pictures show the plain unvarnished reality from which he knew how to find the artistic charm, without regard for

Antoine Watteau, ▶
The Bath of Diana (detail), c. 1715-1716.
Oil on canvas, 80 x 101 cm.
Musée du Louvre, Paris.

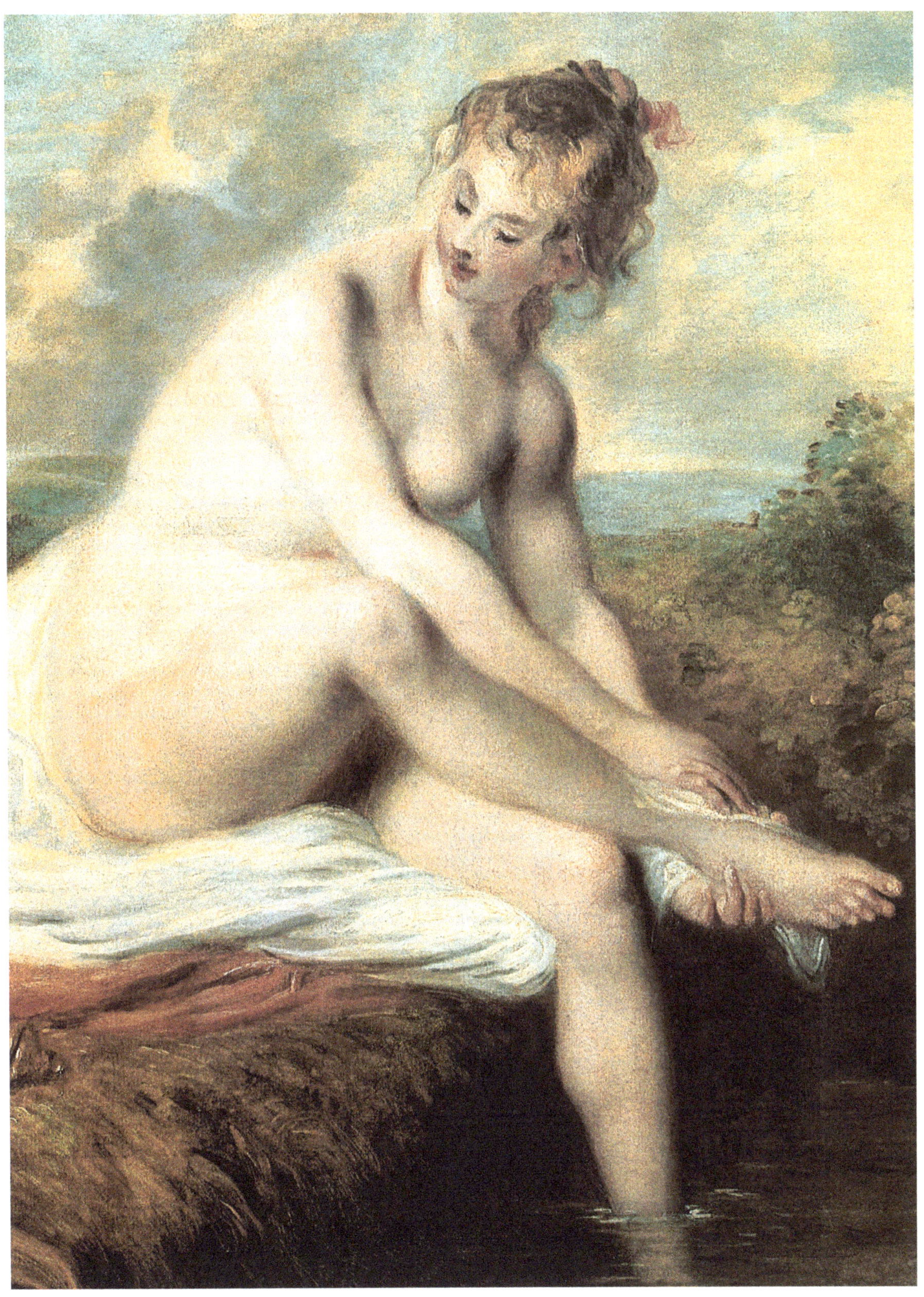

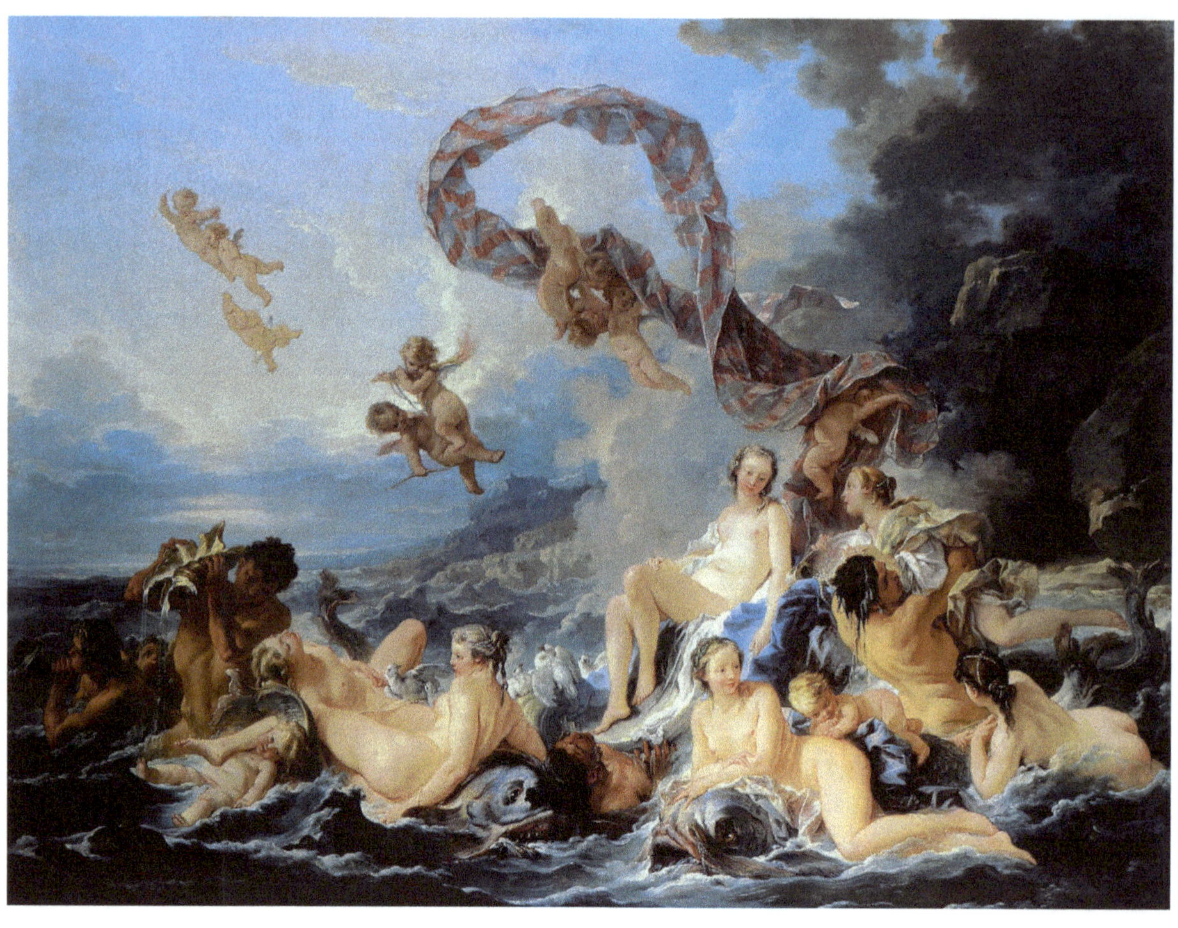

▲ **François Boucher**,
The Triumph of Venus, 1740.
Oil on canvas, 130 x 162 cm.
Nationalmuseum, Stockholm.

particularly intensified intellectual or spiritual profundity in the pictures. In 1728, the Royal Academy accepted two of his new still-life works from this year: *The Skate* and *The Buffet.* This gave him accreditation and membership, allowing him to receive royal commissions. Chardin revealed in oils the hidden poetry and intimacy that lingers behind objects of daily life in addition to capturing their splendour and subtleties. He did not seek his models amongst the rural population, but painted the domestic life of the citizens of Paris. Some of his best works were *The Washerwoman* (1735), *Saying Grace* and *Morning Toilette.*

Jean–Baptiste Greuze (1725-1805) was one of the most significant artists of the French school in the 18th century. His unique style and sentimental, melodramatic genre pictures distinguished him from all the others; he created his own, uniquely

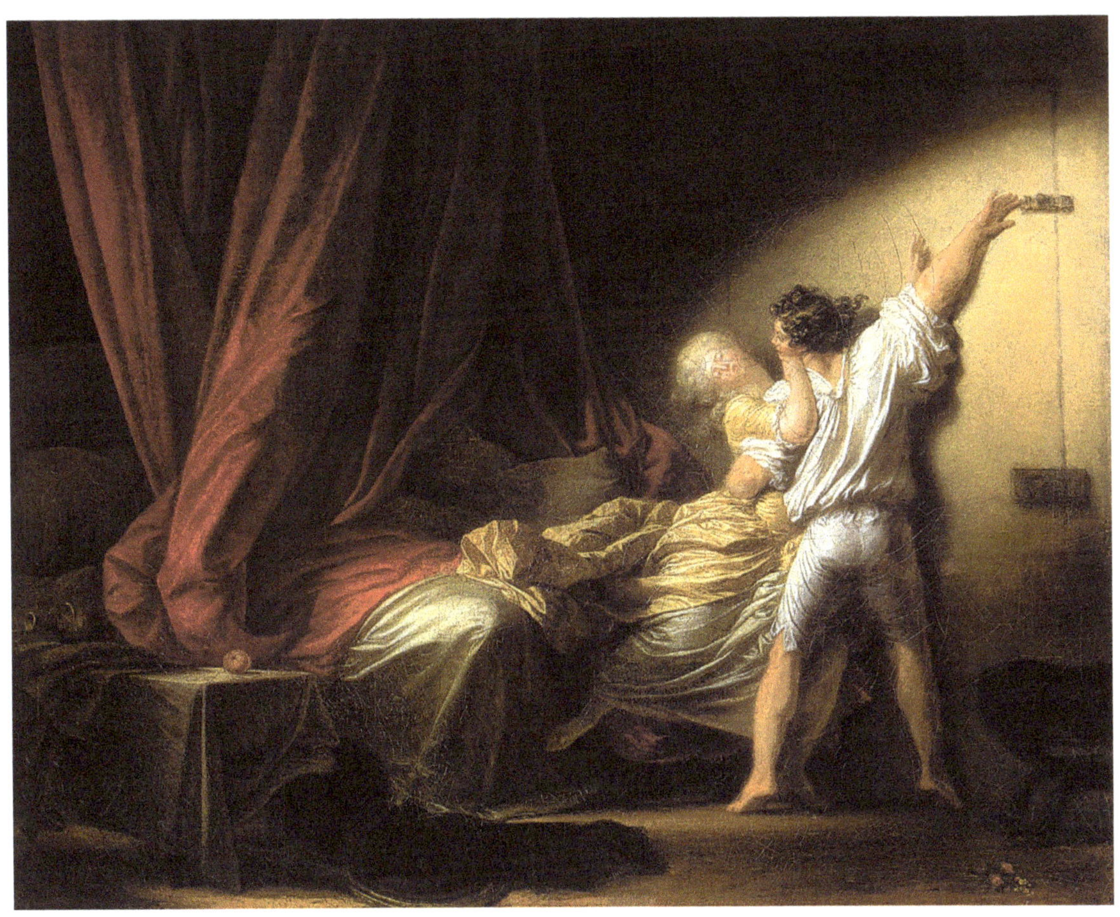

personal style. His *L'Accordee du Village* (1713), *The Village Bride (1761)*, in which every detail had the effect of an actor playing his role, seemed to emerge from a sentimental domestic drama. Many of his later works were delightful pictures of young girls. Greuze placed the emphasis very particularly on the sensitive, even if it then, as in *The Broken Jug* (1785), occasionally crossed the line into the melodramatic. In the representation of faces and half-figures of pretty children and girls, sometimes looking rather lost in thought but also fitting the taste of the upper classes, he made certain admissions, whereby he created a style of painting which has outlived all the revolutionary upheavals. These works include the *Portrait of a Young Peasant Girl* and *Portrait of a Young Girl* (both c. 1770-1780). With the end of the century, his career, too, came to an end. A new style and a new star were discovered: neoclassicism and Jacques-Louis David.

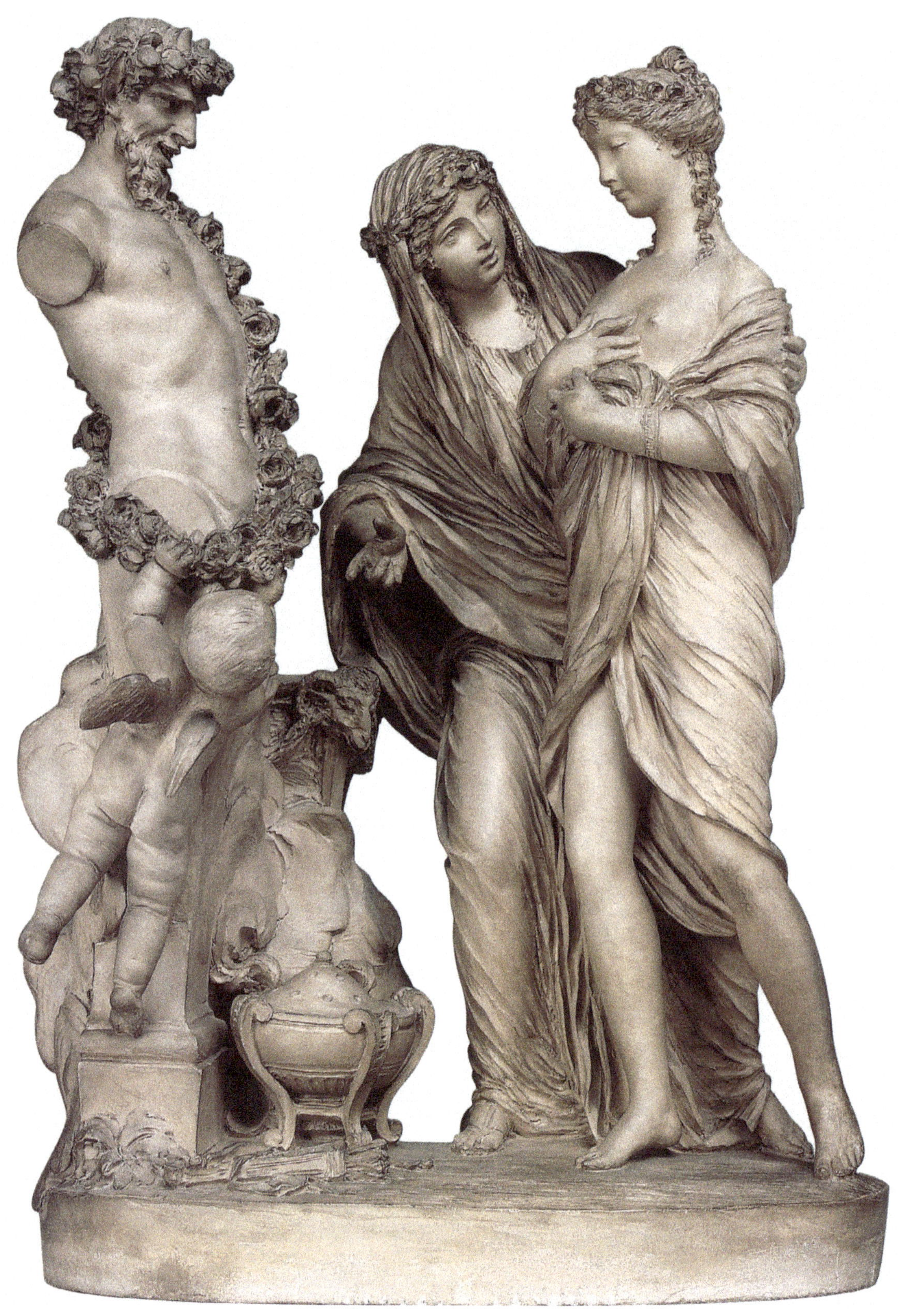

Sculpture

France in the 18th century held a leading role in the fine arts. With the death of the Sun King and the end of Absolutism, a change in the tastes of French patrons became clear: they were now looking for a less grandiose style. For sculpture, ideally suited to interior decoration, this was the birth of Rococo.

Yet this graceful life ended abruptly when the ideas of the Enlightenment emerged from the French Revolution of 1789. The bloody events put an end to the frivolous French Rococo style; tastes now inclined towards strict, puritanical classicism. Only the great monumental sculpture still followed the old paths in the 18th century. Its most respective representative was Jean-Baptiste Pigalle, whose *Monument to the Marshal of Saxony* in St. Thomas Church in Strasbourg clearly exhibits the pompous, theatrical, fundamental characteristics of Baroque. Much more joyful, on the other hand, are the frequently less noticed works of genre sculpture which retain ties to

◀ **Clodion (Claude Michel),**
Vestal Presenting a Young Woman at the Altar of Pan, c. 1770-1775.
Terracotta, height: 43.2 cm.
J. Paul Getty Museum, Los Angeles.

nature and reality: for example, the fountain relief with children playing and allegories of the seasons of Edmé Bouchardon.

Edmé Bouchardon (1698 –1762) was regarded in his time as one of the greatest sculptors; in 1722 he won the Prix de Rome. He really turned against the Baroque tradition of Gian Lorenzo Bernini. He was not strongly in favour of the playful Rococo and instead leaned more towards classicism. During his ten-year stay in Rome he created a remarkable bust of Pope Benedict XIII.

The masterpiece that established his reputation was *Cupid Cutting His Bow from the Club of Hercules.* The two other famous works are the fountain in the Rue de Grenelle in Paris and the statue of Louis XV on horseback (1748) commissioned by the city of Paris. During the ceremonial unveiling, the statue was praised as the most beautiful work of its kind that had ever been created in France. In fact, Bouchardon was not given time to finish it – this task was taken on by Pigalle. Later the monument fell victim to the Revolution and was destroyed.

Nicolas Coustou (1658-1733) and **Guillaume Coustou the Elder** (1677-1746) were the sons of a woodcutter in Lyon. At age 23 Nicolas won the Prix-Colbert, which enabled him to study for four years at the Académie de France in Rome. He was then appointed Chancellor and Director of the Académie Royale in Paris. From 1690, he worked along with Coysevox on the furnishing of the Palaces of Marly and Versailles. He had an unusual talent and his numerous works, which include *La Seine et la Marine* (c. 1712), an *Apollo* (1713-1714) and *Louis XV as Jupiter* (1725), are nevertheless some of the most representative examples of his era and can still be admired today.

His younger brother Guillaume was an even better sculptor. He won the Prix-Colbert as well, but did not want to subject himself to the rules of the Académie. For a while he led the life of a homeless person on the streets of Rome. Finally, the sculptor Pierre Le Gros employed him in his workshop. Like his brother he was in the service of the Sun King, Louis XIV. His most beautiful work is the *Horse Restrained by a Groom*, one of the equestrian statues in Marly-le-Roi, which may now be seen as copies on the Champs-Élysées in Paris. Coustou, also worked for the Prussian King Frederick II, for whom he created the statues *Mars* and *Venus*.

Antoine Coysevox (1640-1720), one of the greatest of all French sculptors, came from a family of Spanish origin. As a seventeen-year-old he created his first statue, a wonderful Madonna. At the request of Louis XIV in 1671, he created a series of monuments for the royal gardens and many interior decorations. Because of his services to art he was accepted in 1676 as a member of the Académie Royale. He received the commission to make statues of Louis XIV and Charlemagne, which even today may still be admired in the Church of St. Louis-des-Invalides in Paris. Probably his most brilliant works include *La Renommée* (Fame) at the entrance to the Tuileries, a sculpted group with a winged horse ridden by Fama (1699-1702) and *Mercury* (1701-1702), the tomb of Jean-Baptiste Colbert in the church of St. Eustace and the tomb of Cardinal Jules Mazarin (1689-1693). Coysevox was an excellent sculptor even if, in accord with the tastes of the age, he was somewhat pompous and exaggerated.

Jean-Antoine Houdon (1741-1823) entered the Royal Academy of Sculpture at the age of twelve. At twenty, after he had learned everything which René-Michel Slodtz and Jean-Baptiste Pigalle could teach him, he won the Prix de Rome, where he worked for the next ten years. His immense talent was enthusiastically embraced by Pope Clement XIV. When seeing his *St. Bruno* for the Church of Santa Maria degli Angeli, the Pope is said to have cried out: "he would speak if he were not bound by the rules of the Order!" Houdon sent his *Morpheus* (1771) for exhibition in the Salon, which guaranteed him affiliation to the Académie Royale de Sculpture. He created the portrait busts of Denis Diderot, Catherine of Russia (1773) and Prince Golitsyn which were exhibited in the Salon of 1773.

Houdon also devoted himself intensively to his work as a teacher at the Académie. During anatomy

Guillaume Coustou, ▶
Horse Restrained by a Groom,
also known as *the Marly Horse,* 1739-1745.
Carrara marble, 340 x 284 x 127 cm.
Musée du Louvre, Paris.

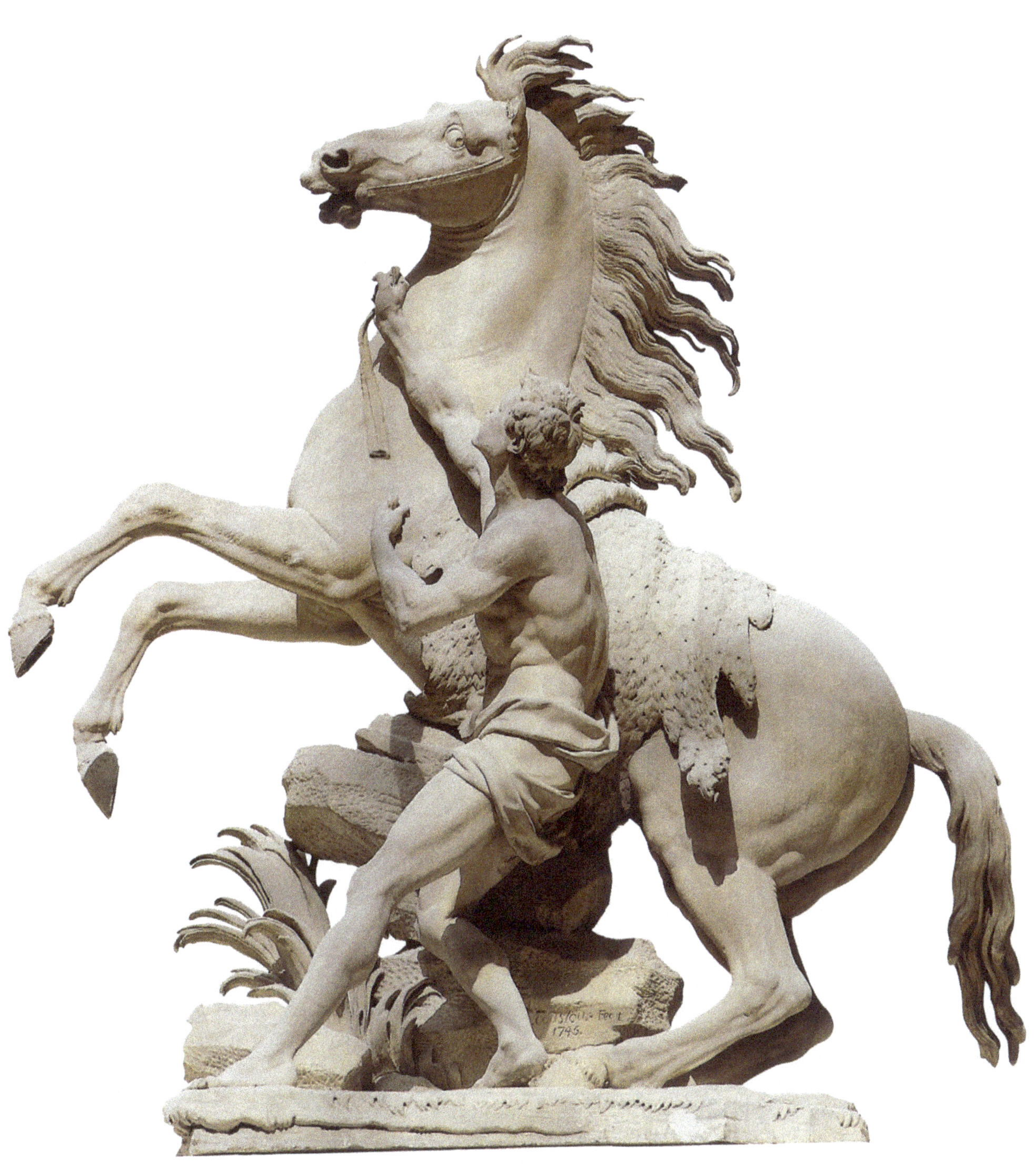

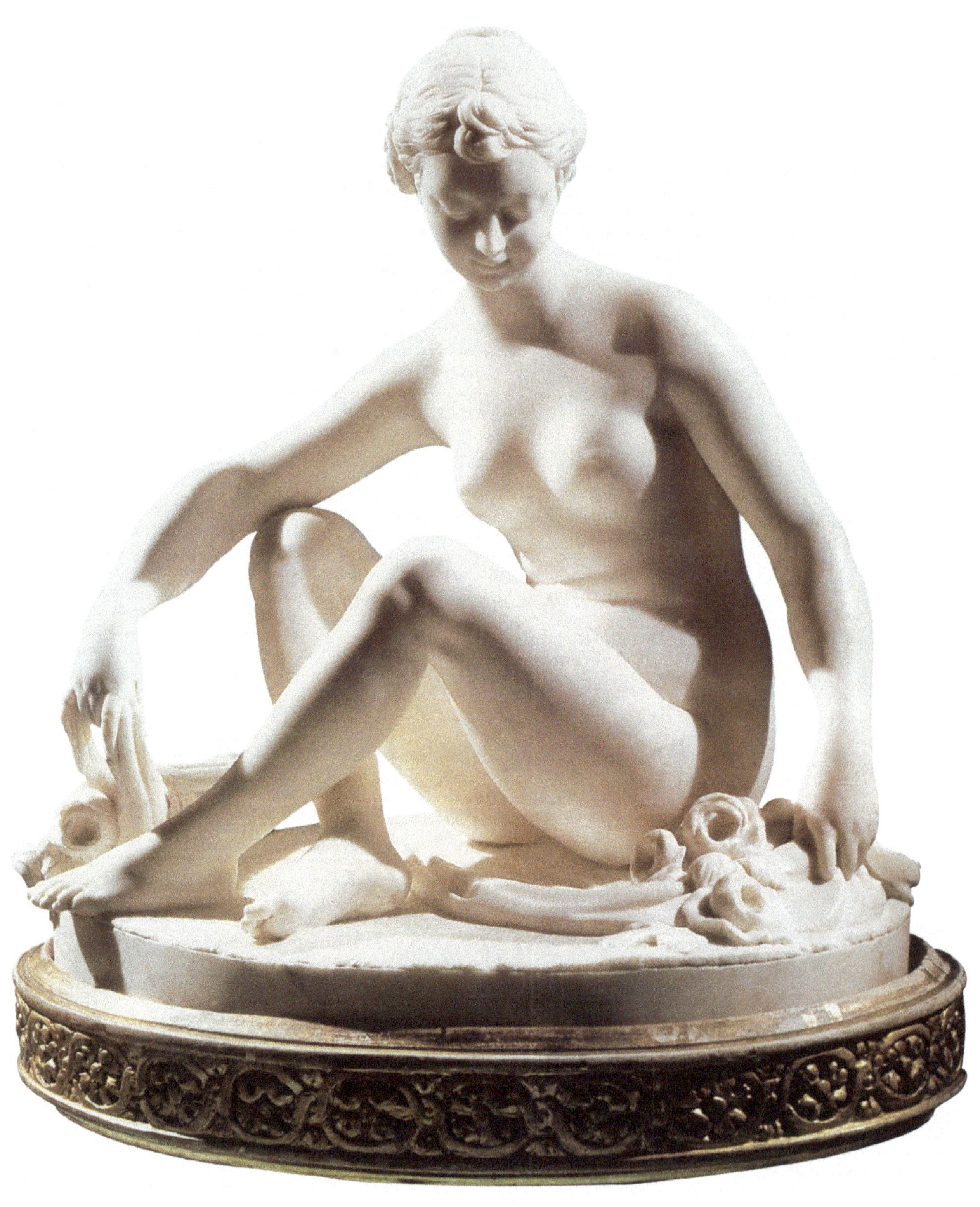

lessons, he utilised his *Flayed Man* as an example for his students, and this picture is currently still used for the same purpose. In the drawing rooms of society, he was a very welcome guest; most of the leading personalities of the age sat for him as subjects. His busts are amazingly lifelike portraits. In 1783 the artist travelled to America to complete a statue of George Washington, of whom he had already modelled a bust in 1778. In Washington, D.C., he was a guest of the President at Mount Vernon. The statue was intended for the capitol in the State of Virginia.

After his return to France, Houdon finished *The Chilly Woman* for the King of Prussia as a contrasting piece to a summer statue, a naïve embodiment of a shivering, freezing figure of winter, one of his best and most famous works. Finally, the outbreak of the Revolution put an abrupt end to this chain of commissions. During the time of Napoleon, there was hardly anything for Houdon to do, yet he received the commission for a colossal relief to decorate the column in honour of the Grande Armée in Boulogne and for several busts, including one of Marshal Ney (1806) and one of Josephine and Napoleon. After his wife died in 1823, Houdon withdrew further from the limelight. In addition, he suffered from arteriosclerosis, and he died, somewhat isolated, five years after his wife.

Jean-Baptiste Pigalle (1714–1785) was the son of a royal ebony artist, an artistic cabinet maker whose main working material was ebony, which was dark, hard and difficult to work with. He joined the workshop of Robert Lerrain as an apprentice and then became a pupil of Jean-Baptiste Lemoyne. In the competition for the Prix de Rome he was unsuccessful; therefore, probably around 1740, he set off on foot and penniless for Rome and lived there in extremely impoverished conditions. This might have cost him his life if the sculptor Guillaume Coustou had not taken him in.

The French Ambassador in Rome was so impressed with Pigalle's work that he bought a copy of the *Card Player* from him. After his return to Paris, he created the marble statuette *Mercury Fastening His Sandals,* which he submitted as his application for membership to the Academy. The King bought a copy in larger format and commissioned a second statue, a Venus (1748). In addition, Pigalle received a whole series of commissions via his patron Madame de Pompadour. She gave him the commission for the portrait of Louis XV in Bellevue (destroyed) and a sculpture with the title *Love and Friendship* (1758). In the allegorical *Madame de Pompadour as Friendship,* Pigalle beautifully portrayed his patron.

Pigalle also enjoyed the favour of the Marquise de Marigny, who was instrumental in obtaining for him the commission for the mausoleum of Marshal Maurice de Saxe. In addition to his monumental sculptures, Pigalle also distinguished himself as a creator of busts and statuettes. His works, particularly in later years, are marked by strongly naturalistic features, as for example the *Nude Voltaire.* Also his figures of children are of exceptional quality, for example the famous *Boy with the Birdcage* (1749).

◄ **Étienne-Maurice Falconet**,
Flora, c. 1751.
Marble, height: 32 cm.
The State Hermitage Museum, St. Petersburg.

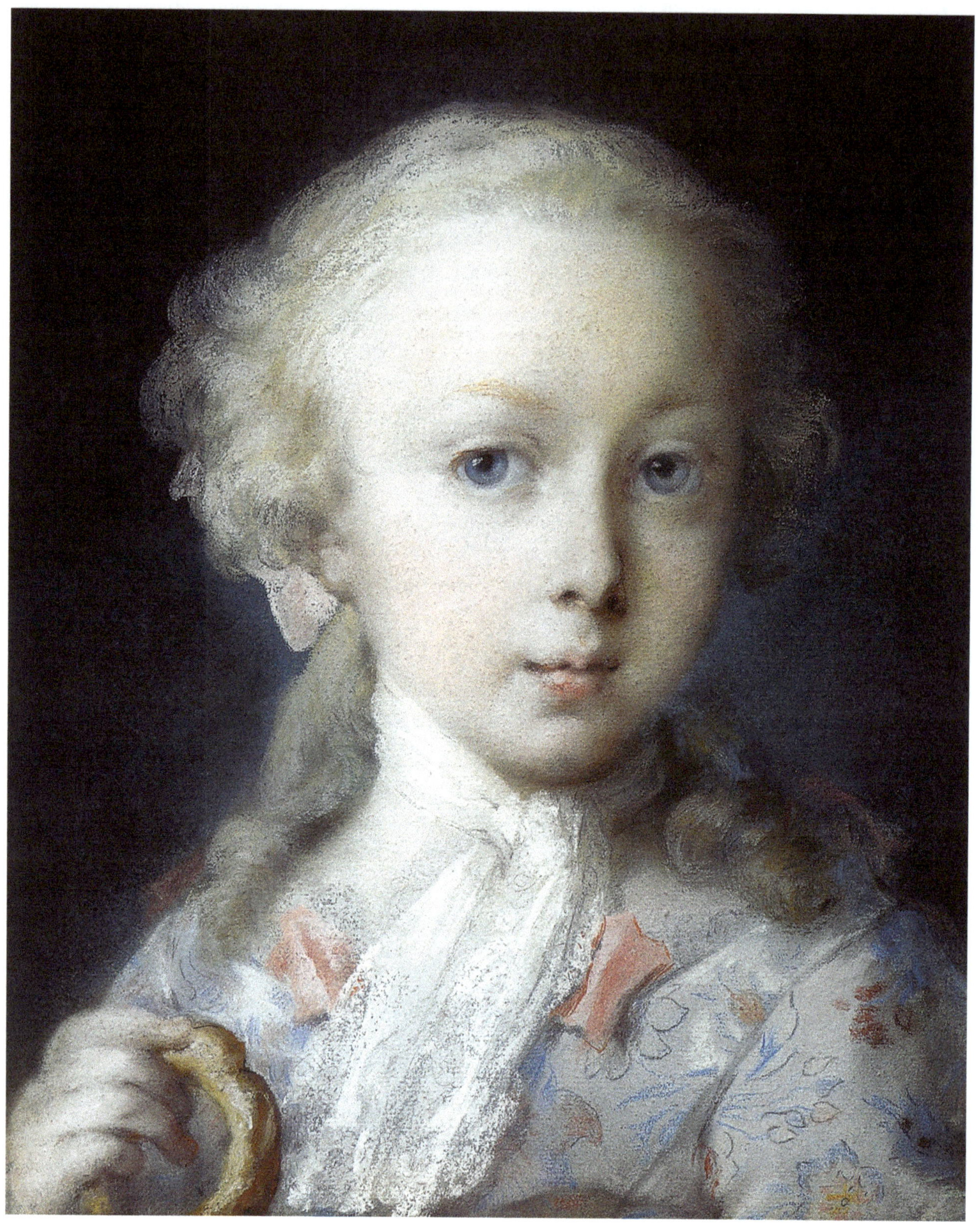

ROCOCO IN ITALY

talian Rococo society appears strange to us today, powdered, polished, always politely bowing to each other, but shooting the arrows of poisoned verses with loving delight. At first sight, nothing but decay could be seen, but these new ideas were like a raging storm that seemed to tear away everything that had been created in the previous centuries.

It has often been said that the birthplace of the Baroque was the palace of Madame de Pompadour. But even in those days it was scarcely in the boudoirs or bedrooms of the mighty that cultural trends emerged. Rococo originated where Baroque decayed. And the influence of Asia on the emergence of Rococo must not be underestimated. Above all, the Jesuit scholar Athanasius Kircher familiarised Italian artists with the secrets of Asian art, An oriental haze hovered even above painting, in which strange-seeming figures were brought to life in Tiepolo's frescoes.

Overall, however, Italy in the 18th century found itself in a period of decline. But there is no mistaking the fact that the Italians, despite economic crises and political pressure, had preserved a great store of creative power and played an energetic part in Europe's cultural life.

◀ **Rosalba Carriera,**
Portrait of a Boy in the Leblond Family, 1740.
Pastel on paper, 34 x 27 cm.
Gallerie dell'Accademia, Venice.

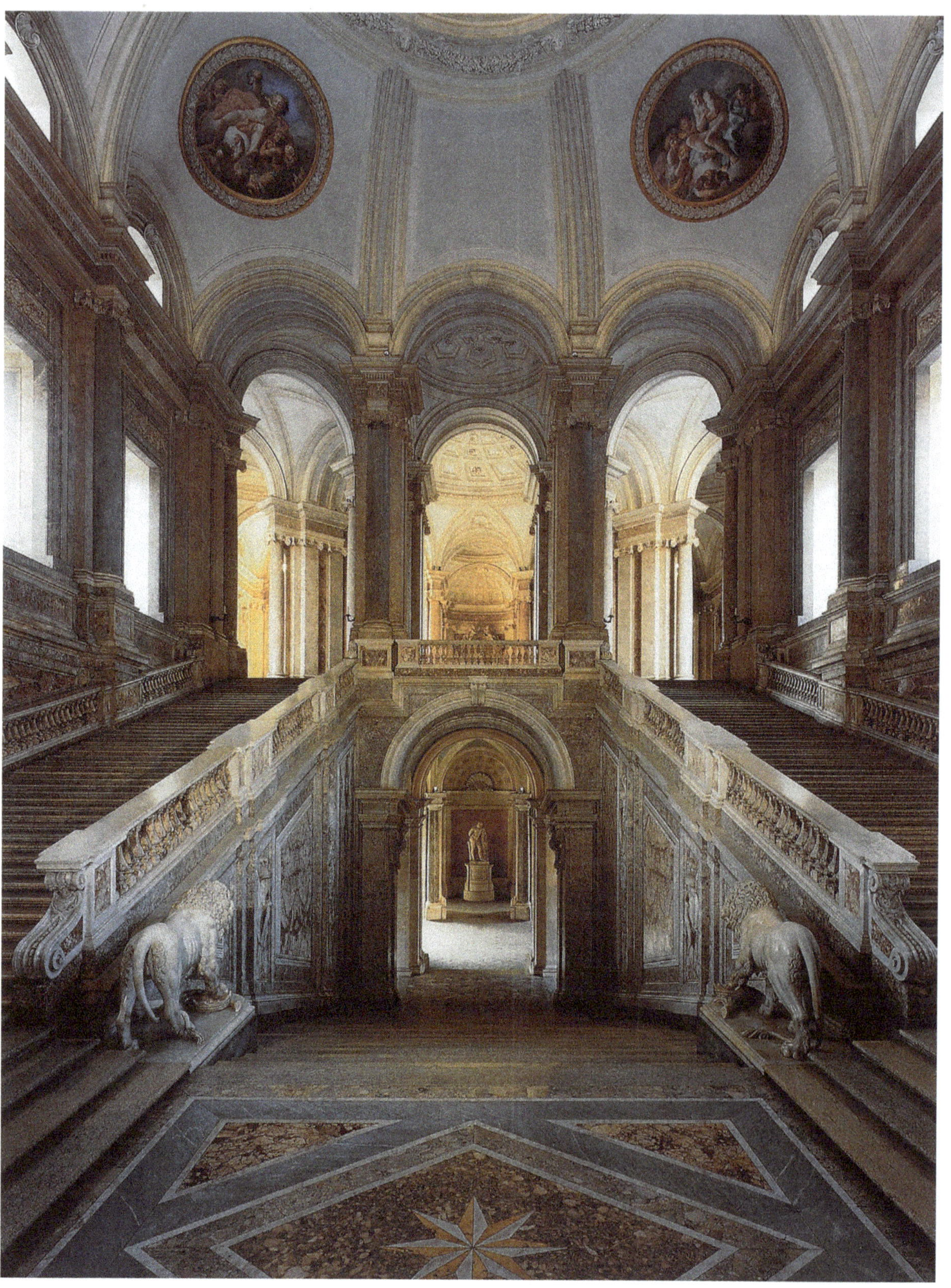

Architecture

With Gian Lorenzo Bernini, Carlo Fontana, Francesco Borromini, the great competitor of Bernini, and Baldassare Longhena, Italy had found its appropriate forms of architecture. The influence of these masters was so strong that even the following generations adopted at least some of their precepts.

It was Francesco Borromini who in his sketches banned all straight lines and replaced them with curves and twirls, removing all significance from the basic shapes and giving greater importance to decorations. The best-known of the successors are Filippo Juvarra and Luigi Vanvitelli, who with the castle in Caserta introduced into Italy the French style of palace building, with its considerable extensions, and this removed Italy's isolation, maintained up until this point, from the architecture of other countries.

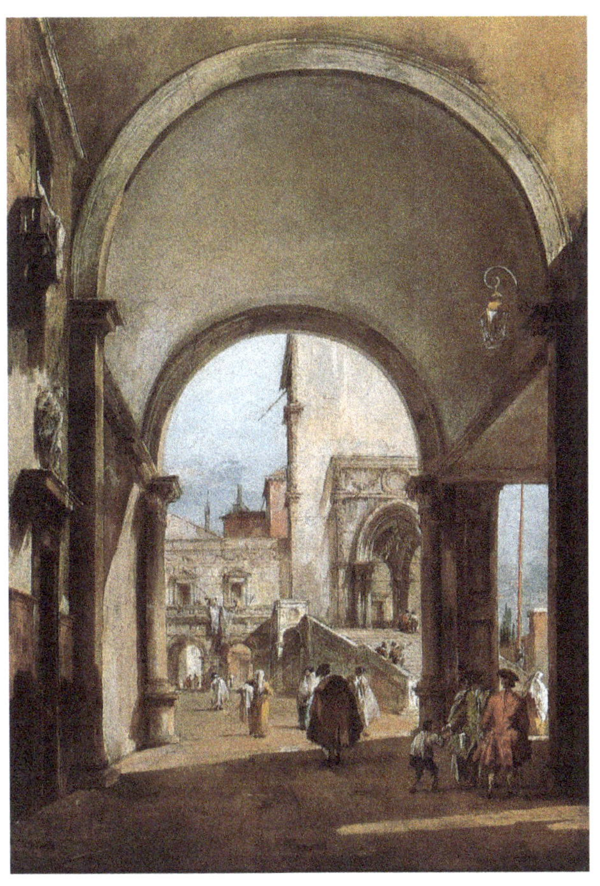

◀ **Luigi Vanvitelli**,
Royal Palace, Main Stairs, 1751-1780.
Reggia di Caserta, Caserta.

▲ **Francesco Guardi**,
An Architectural Caprice, c. 1770.
Oil on canvas, 54.2 x 36.2 cm.
The National Gallery, London.

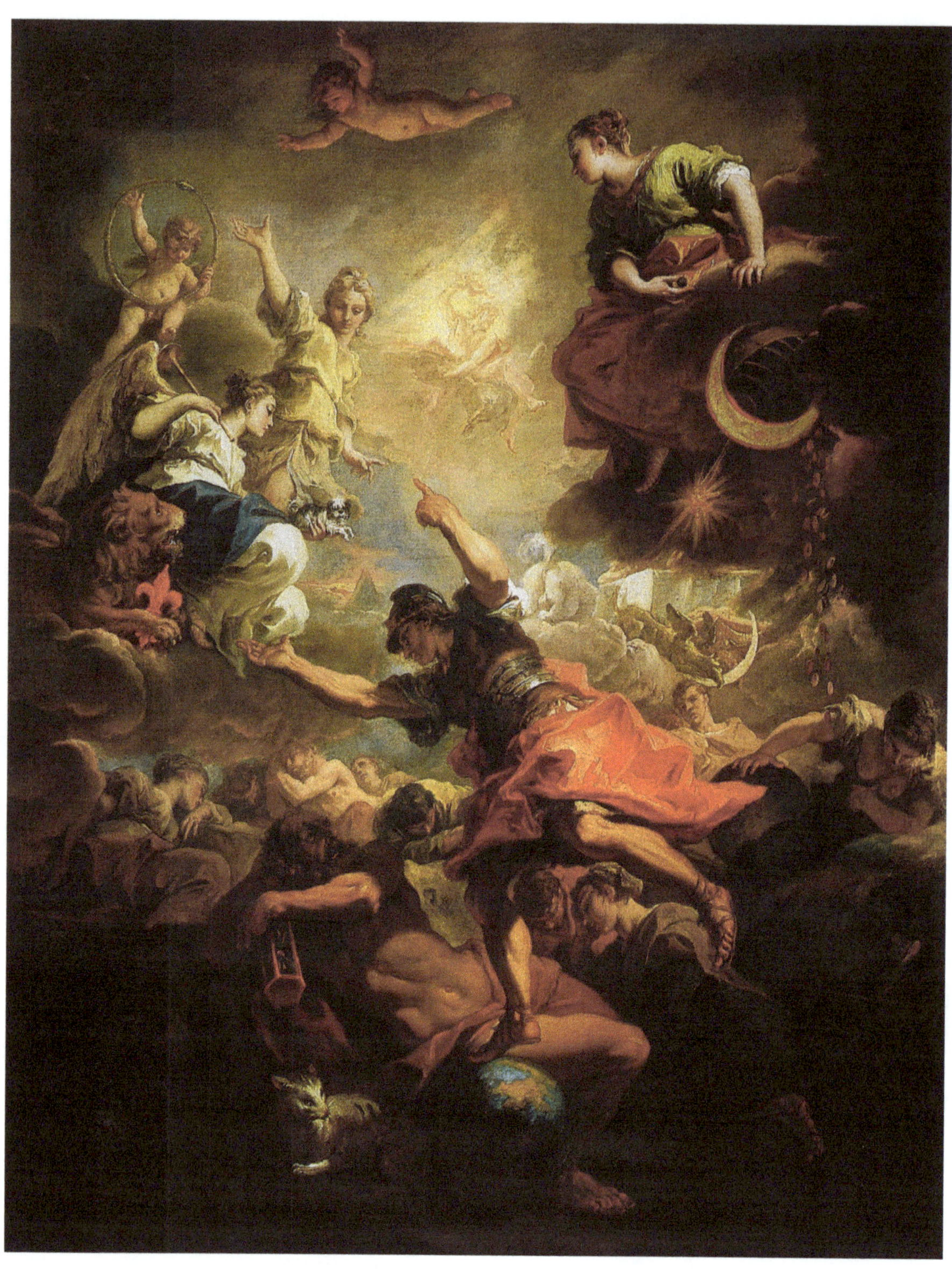

▲ **Sebastiano Ricci**, *Allegory of Tuscany,* 1706.
Oil on canvas, 90 x 70.5 cm. Galleria degli Uffizi, Florence.

Painting

The movement towards simplicity and nature began to emanate into the art world, as the style once again returned to the Old Masters. In these years, Rome was the epicentre of all artistic endeavours, but in Venice, too, an impressive art scene was again beginning to develop. The character of Venetian painting in the 18th century was determined by the artists, who strove to accurately depict society. Three of the most famous painters in Venice were without doubt Francesco Guardi, Pietro Longhi and Canaletto.

Canaletto (1697 – 1768) is the oldest in this group of famous Venetian painters. His name can be traced back to his views of Venetian canals with their adjacent churches and palaces, and who thus created a special kind of architectural painting. He began his career, just like his father, as a painter of scenery for the stage. He moved to Rome at the age of twenty, and stayed there for the rest of his life. Canaletto had many pupils, including Jean-Honoré Fragonard. He specialised initially in *veduta*, maintaining loyalty to the spectacular views of his hometown of Venice. Typical of his work was the contrast between light and shadow. Many of his views were simply pictures of the city, while others were depictions of celebrations or ceremonies.

The most important features of the paintings of Canaletto are the atmosphere, the local colour, and the geometrical perspective. Amongst his unsurpassed views of Venice are his two views of *Il Canale Grande* (1730-1750) and two views of *Il Canale Grande a Rialto* (1730-1750), the Piazza San Marco painted over and over again between 1720 and 1750. In London, in the period between 1746 and 1755, he created not only views of the Thames but also of Windsor Castle, and paintings for the gallery of the Duke of Richmond. Canaletto's masterpieces influenced the entire sphere of landscape painting in the 19th century.

These works were later expanded upon by his nephew, also called Canaletto, Bernardo Bellotto, who connected so closely with the style of his uncle that many of their works can scarcely be differentiated from one another.

Pietro Longhi (1701-1785) captivated his audience more by his humour than by his drawing and colouring skills. He was responsible for such magnificent pictures as *The Happy Couple* (c. 1740), the *Family Concert* (c. 1752), the *Lady with her Dressmaker* (c. 1760), *The Hairdresser* (c. 1760). His inherently perceptive nature can be observed within *The Faint* (c. 1744), *The Temptation* (c. 1750), *The Geography Lesson* (c. 1752) and *The Alchemists* (c. 1757). Occasionally Longhi is described as a Venetian William Hogarth. However, nothing bound them together but an approximately parallel lifetime: the desire to paint and the style of painting set them distinctly apart – the one satirically sharp and the other soft, cheerful and acquiescent.

Francesco Guardi (1712-1793) studied under Canaletto, and painted with similarly light brush strokes. He achieved his effects of light and air with a delicate sketching technique; scarcely anyone understood better than himself how to reproduce reflecting lights on water, and how to leave out details in favour of creating an overall impression. An example of this is the *Venetian Gala Concert* which appears almost impressionistic. Guardi's colour was at times quite hard and dry, but in terms of truth and accuracy his scenes were comprehensive, even if he did not always strive to give the architectural lines a photographic accuracy.

Amongst his many city views are the *Grand Canal in San Geremia Seen from a Gondola Mooring Place* (c. 1741), the *View of Venice with Santa Maria della Salute and the Dogana* (c. 1780), the *Doge's Palace in Venice* (mid-18th century) and the *Veduta of the Grand Canal between Santa Lucia and the Scalzi* (mid-18th century).

Giovanni Battista Tiepolo (1696-1770) was the last of the great Venetian decorative artists and the finest representative of Italian Rococo. His father Domenico was captain of a merchant vessel; when his father died, his mother sent young Giambattista to Gregorio Lazzarini to serve his apprenticeship. Highly gifted, by the age of twenty Tiepolo was already incredibly well respected in Venice as an artist, painting mainly large, decorative pictures for churches and palaces, and was appointed in 1755 to be the first president of the Venice Academy.

Tiepolo became a star, and cities like Milan, Bergamo, Udine and Vicenza fought for his services. His fame, however, soon made its way northwards, far beyond the Alps to Würzburg. The Prince Elector there funded his journey, which cost an incredible sum of 3000 guilders. In order to get Tiepolo to decorate his palace, a further salary of 21,000 guilders was agreed upon. We can still admire in the Residence Palace in Würzburg the murals, the ceiling paintings, the paintings in the Staircase and the Imperial Hall with a grandiose representation of the four corners of the world, a dazzling work of decorative painting.

Tiepolo's skill in drawing and composition, in his arrangement of groups, depiction and colouration has scarcely been surpassed. Amongst his works are, for example, the *Rape of Europa* (1720-1722), *Alexander the Great* and *Campaspe in the Workshop of Apelles* (1725-1726), *Abraham and the Angels* (1732), *Danae and Zeus* (c. 1736). Amongst the frescoes in the Royal Palace in Madrid are the *Glorification of Spain*, the *Apotheosis of the Spanish Royal Family* (1762-1766) and the *Immaculate Conception* (1767-1768).

The Golden Age of the Venetian artistic tradition came to an end with Tiepolo. He never saw Venice again, and died on March 27, 1770, in Madrid.

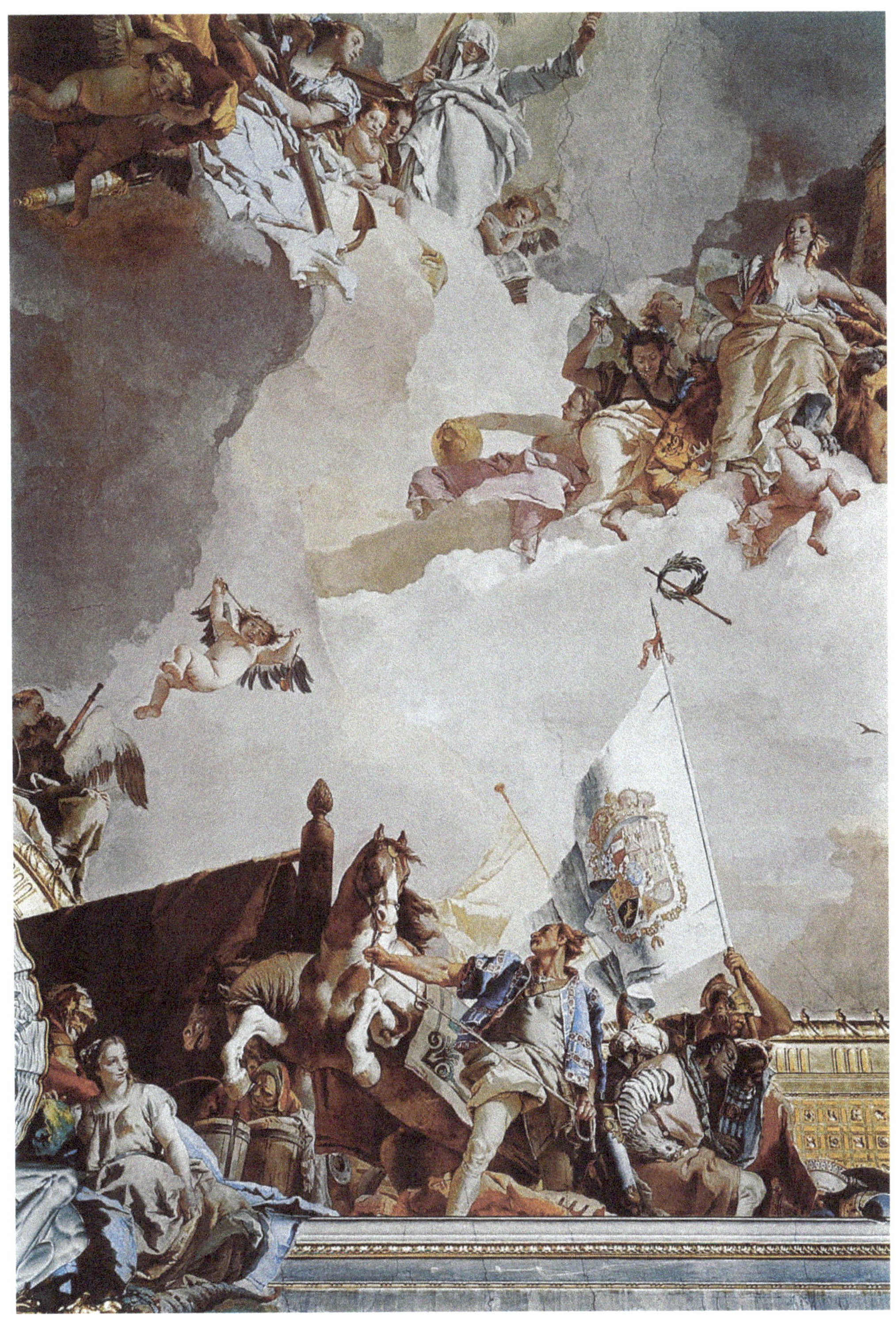

▲ **Giovanni Battista Tiepolo**, *Glorification of Spain*, 1762-1766.
Fresco, 1500 x 900 cm. Palacio Real, Madrid.

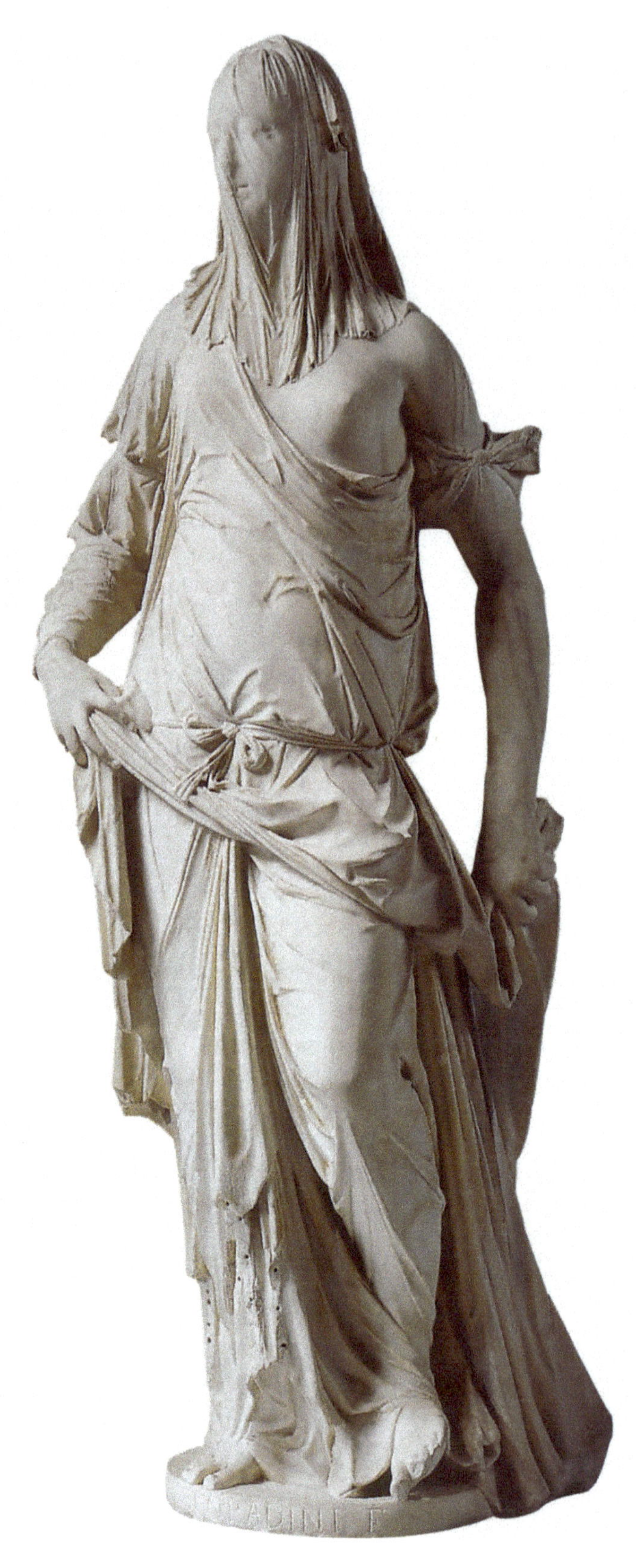

Sculpture

Amongst the Italian sculptors of the 18th century, two stand out quite particularly: Antonio Canova and Nicola Salvi .

Antonio Canova (1757-1822) was the son of a poor stonemason; Canova's father died at an early age, and the boy was raised by his grandfather who wanted him to continue the family tradition of stone masonry. To draw from a nice anecdote, Canova's career began in the kitchen of a Venetian senator. Legend has it that while preparing a dinner, he shaped the butter into a winged Venetian lion and brought it to the table. The guests were enthusiastic and called the ten-year-old boy into the dining room, expressing their admiration for his work. The hosting senator consequently persuaded the grandfather to offer Antonio an apprenticeship with the sculptor Torretti.

Canova's first commission consisted of statues of Orpheus and Eurydice (1776), which were to be erected on the steps of his patron's palace. These two statues were followed by the group *Daedalus and Icarus*. In 1780, he went to Rome, where he turned his attention to the works of classical art. Well-known works from this period are *Psyche Revived by Cupid's Kiss* and his bare-knuckled fighters *Damoxenes and Creugas*. During his stay he started one of his masterpieces: *Theseus Conquers the Minotaur* (1805-1819). Amongst his admirers was Napoleon, who gave him an important commission for a colossal bust. Canova was made Imperial Sculptor and created portraits of Napoleon's mother Marie-Louise, his sister Pauline as Venus Victrix (1805-1808) and many other members of the court.

In Vienna, he received the commission to create a monument for the Mausoleum of the Archduchess Marie Christine of Austria (1798-1805). Probably his most famous portrait is the bust of Pope Pius VII (1807). The Pope then consulted him about the title of Marquis of Ischia, whereupon Canova planned an enormous statue, called *Religion*. Numerous other commissioned works followed, including famous masterpieces such as *Venus and Mars* (1816-1822). Canova found his final residence in the town of his birth, Possagno. He was regarded as the forerunner of the classical style, who introduced the return to classical ideals and to a more naturalistic interpretation.

◀ **Antonio Corradini,**
Veiled Woman (Faith?), first half of the 18th century.
Marble, 138 x 48 x 36 cm.
Musée du Louvre, Paris.

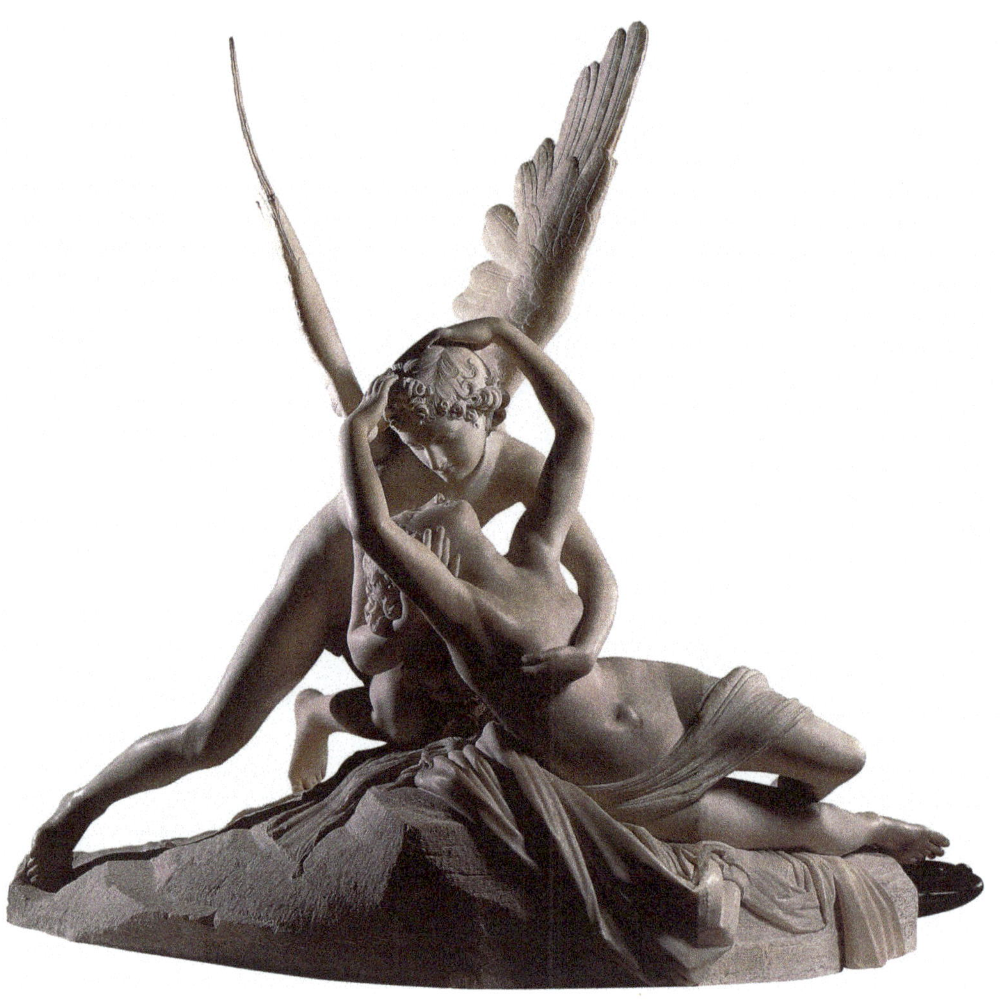

Nicola Salvi (1696-1751), born in Rome, received from Pope Clemens XII the commission to complete the Trevi Fountain, which had been started in 1640 by Bernini. The fountain, placed at the rear of the Palazzo Poli, overwhelms the little square where it is located. This monumental work, with its triumphal arch, beautiful fountains and sparkling lights represents a quintessential example of 18th century Baroque art in Rome. This commission occupied Salvi for a large part of his professional career, and yet he could not finish it. In parallel with it he created, together with Vanvitelli, the chapel of San Giovanni Battista (1742) in the church of Sant' Antonio dei Portoghesi and the façade of the Palazzo Chigi-Odescalchi (1745). In the final years of his life, Salvi became so ill with arthritis that he had to be escorted from place to place in a sedan chair.

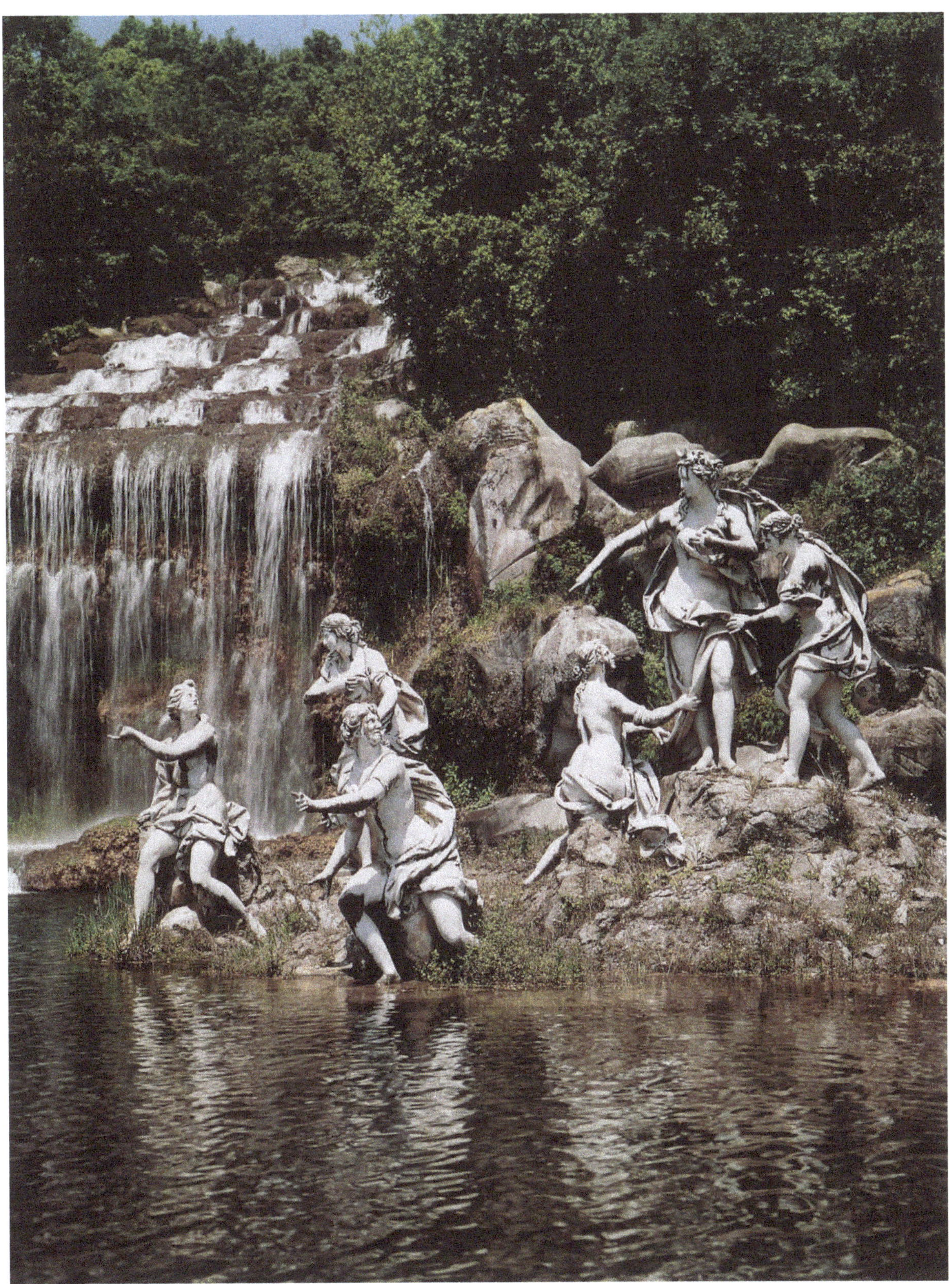

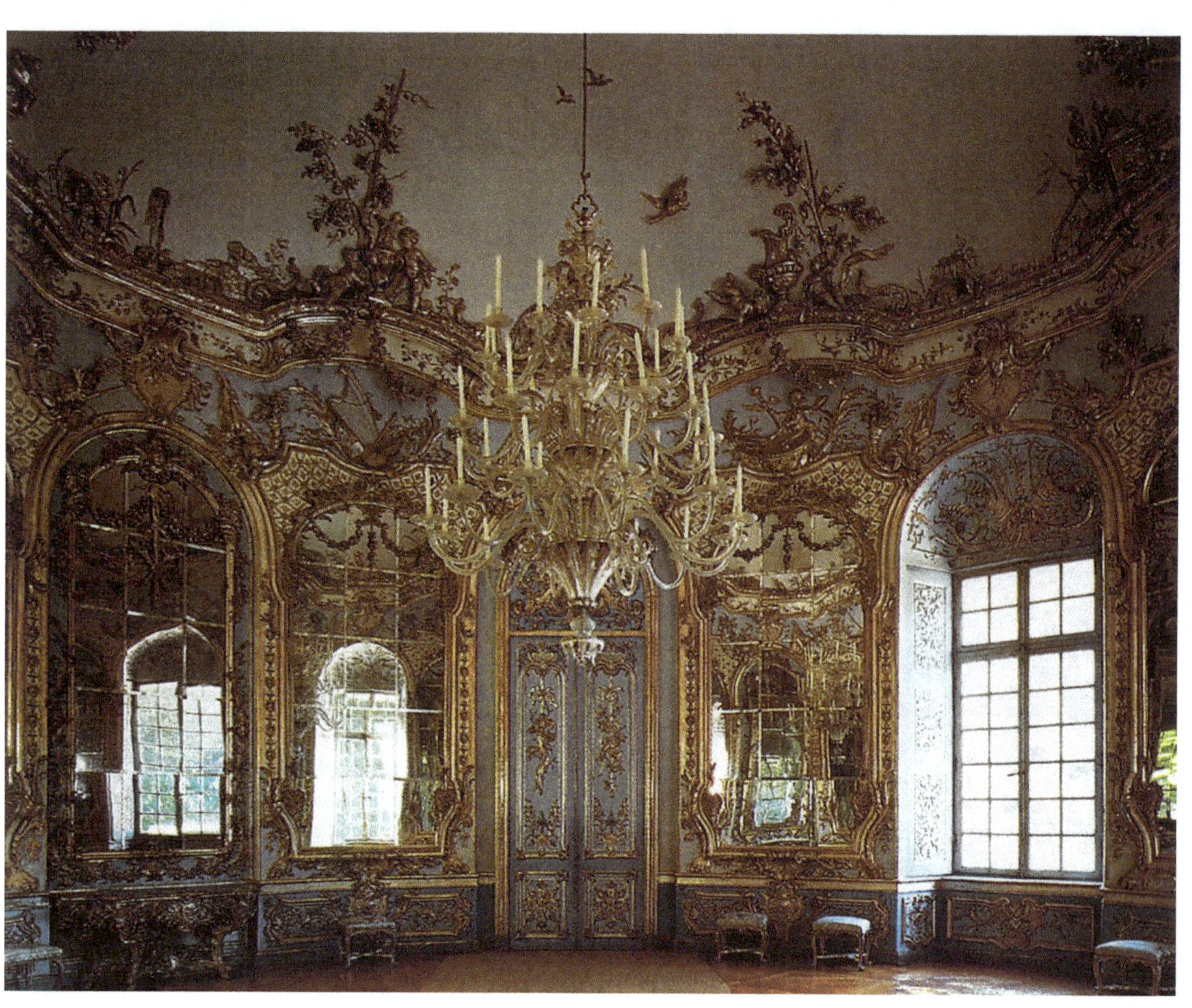

ROCOCO IN GERMANY AND AUSTRIA

Before and during the Seven Years' War (1756-1763) between Prussia and Austria, artistic activity in Germany came to a halt. Painters sought inspiration from fellow artists from other countries. Many courts encouraged the adaptation of French styles and trends, for example in Bavaria, where the palace in Schleissheim and the Schloss Nymphenburg emulated several French models of interior decor and furnishings. French, Italian and Dutch influences often coexisted within one work of art. But French tastes dominated everything. The Academies built along French lines naturally summoned French academics to become their directors.

Italian architecture, too, left behind many traces in Germany; in particular church architecture followed the precepts of the Vatican. Monasteries and abbeys used their regained power and growth to gratify their passion for building. Particularly in Bavaria and Austria, most monasteries were either built from new or reconstructed under the model of the Roman church in this era. In addition, the towers were embellished with a German detail: onion-shaped imperial roofs.

However, the architecture of the second half of the 18th century can be interpreted as a transition into neoclassicism.

◄ **François de Cuvilliés**,
Amalienburg, Hall of Mirrors, 1734-1739.
Schloss Nymphenburg, Munich.

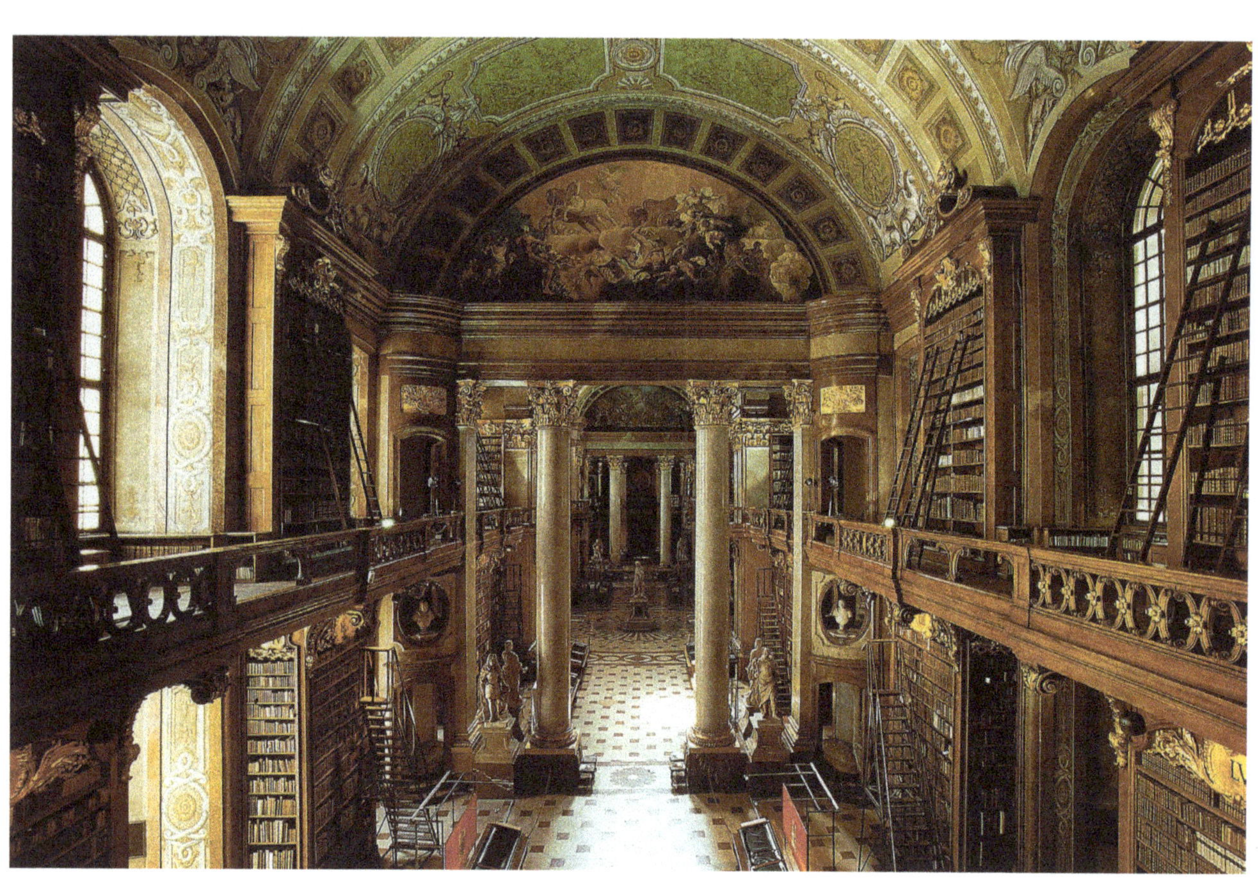

Architecture

Most of the buildings were constructed by secular princes. The residences that were often the central point of artistic efforts epitomised the reawakened passion for architecture which was a sign of the renewed awareness after the turmoil of the Reformation.

Matthäus Daniel Pöppelmann (1662-1736) received in Dresden, from his prince the commission to plan the building of a Zwinger (tower) on the site of a former fortress between the outer and inner wall of fortification. The arrangement was meant to contain "in the style the Roman state, luxury and pleasure buildings". Here above all, in the "show castle", was where the summer revels of the Saxon Court were to take place.

Somewhat tardily, Augustus the Strong in the end had to convert to the Catholic faith in order to become King of Poland, and the Frauenkirche was complemented by the Hofkirche (Royal Court Church), the magnificent Catholic Cathedral of

St. Trinitatis (1739-1754), both the planning and the building of which were part of a cooperative project of a quartet of architects. The project was started by the Italian master builder Gaetano Chiaveri and then completed first by Sebastian Wetzel and Johann Christoph Knöffel and finally by Julius Heinrich Schwarze. Particularly striking is the super elevated central tower, which stands above the main entrance at a height of approximately 85 metres. This church, with the exception of the tower, was also destroyed by the heavy bomb attacks in February 1945 and rebuilt in 1987.

Certainly not in number, but definitely in significance, the buildings of Berlin were in no way inferior to those in Dresden. In Berlin, a spirit prevailed after the assumption of government by Prince Frederick I which differed from all of the other German princely courts. For political and religious reasons, there were strong feelings against France and when the Prince sought to embellish his residence with new buildings and works of art he drew from the artistic resources of the Netherlands and from the circle of Protestants who had fled from France for religious reasons.

◄ **Johann Bernhard Fischer von Erlach**,
Court Library, 1723-1726.
Vienna.

Andreas Schlüter (1660-1714) was an artist in whom the talents of the architect and the sculptor were harmoniously present. The most brilliant evidence of this is the monument of the Great Prince Elector, designed between 1696 and 1697 as the first free-standing equestrian statue in Germany. It was erected in 1703 on the occasion of the King's 46th birthday. It shows the King in a feudal pose as the fearless hero, a symbol of noble strength on a sturdy battle steed. During the Second World War, the statue was removed from its base and stored on a barge anchored on the River Spree. In the freezing cold winter of 1947-1948, the barge sank along with the statue into Lake Tegel and could not be salvaged until 1949. A year later it was taken to the park of the Sanssouci Schloss.

In 1699, Schlüter was summoned to carry out his greatest task when the Prince entrusted him with the direction of the building of Sanssouci. He developed both the north façade on the Lustgarten (Pleasure Garden) and the south front on the Schlossplatz, and above all he created, in the formation of the architectonic structure of the inner courtyard, a masterpiece of sublime perfection. The Prince Elector was then crowned King in Königsberg, and moved into the new Schloss in 1701. The building was transformed into the most Rococo Baroque château and demonstrated the different stance taken by Prussia in comparison with the other German principalities.

Despite all these extraordinary achievements, the King expressed disfavour. Without Schlüter's involvement, a 120-metre-high tower ordered by the King in a fit of building madness was built in an unsuitable location, it then had to be demolished because it threatened to cave in. Because the King still used him only as a stonemason, the enraged Schlüter left Berlin and went to St. Petersburg, where, without being given a single job or commission, he died just one year later in a sad condition.

For the royal Schloss the first commissioner, Prince Elector Frederick II "The Iron" had selected a special building location: the island in the middle of the River Spree. This was a strategically favourable position that gave control over the trade routes from east to west. In the meantime, almost derelict, it was rebuilt and extended beginning in 1699 by Andreas Schlüter and turned into a magnificent château. Only the death of the Prince Elector put an end to the overall planning, and for financial reasons, under King Frederick William I, a more reasonable version of the previous project was completed. Not until the middle of the 19th century was any construction added, for example the building on the cupola. In May 1944, the Schloss was severely damaged by bombing attacks; on the 3rd of February 1945, it burned for four days after further bombing raids.

Georg Wenzeslaus von Knobelsdorff (1699-1753) was the most important architect of King Frederick II the Great who came to the throne of Prussia in 1740. Von

Johann Arnold Nering, ▶
Schloss Charlottenburg,
begun in 1695.
Berlin.

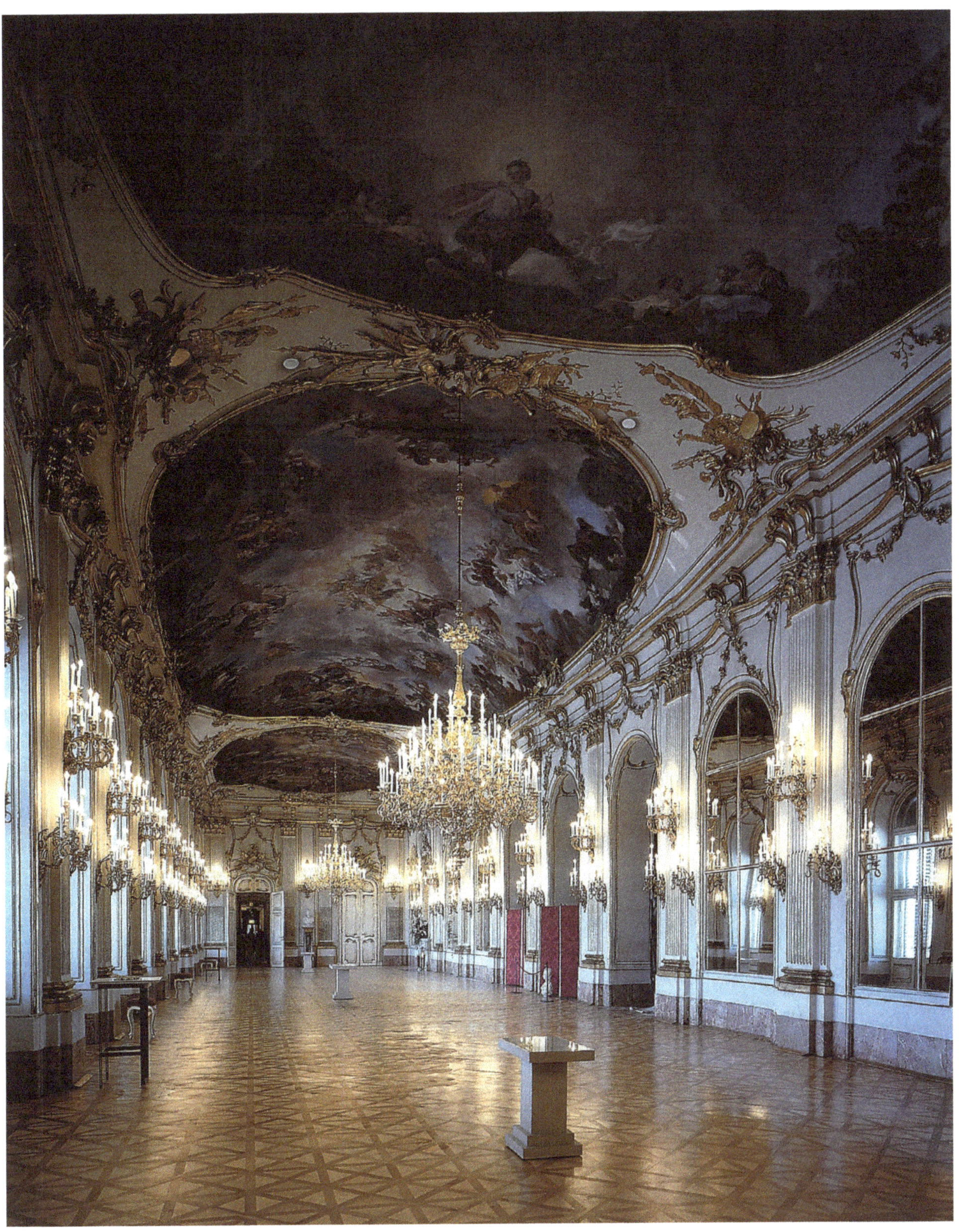

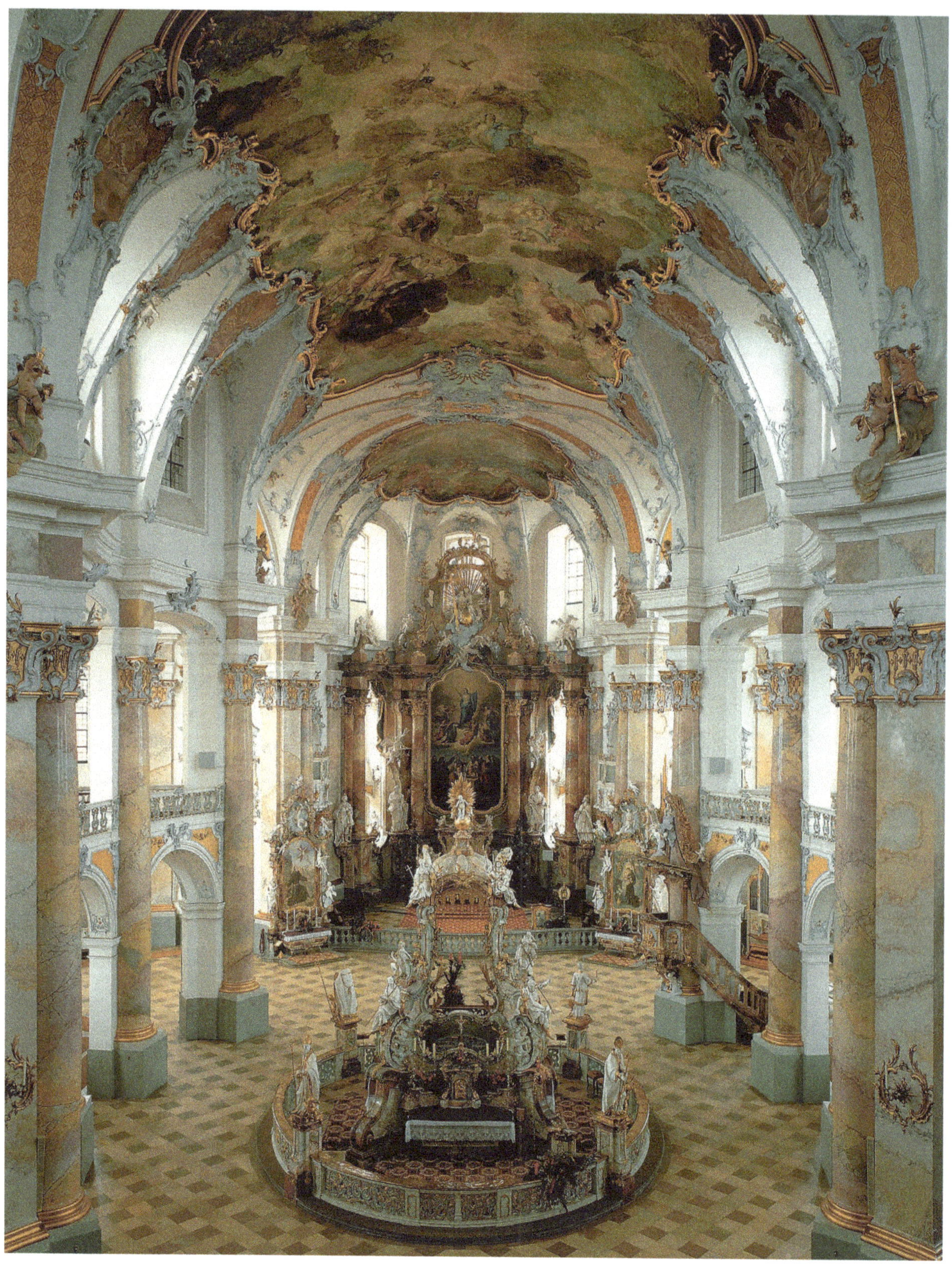

Knobelsdorff was initially an officer but later worked as a painter and landscape architect. One of his first great works was the extension and conversion of the former moat and fortress in Rheinsberg.

King Frederick II wanted a palace in Potsdam, where in the years between 1744 and 1752 the municipal Schloss was converted and the interior extended in Rococo style. The Palace was badly damaged by bombing in the Second World War and rebuilt in late 2013. The interior, which is modern, now houses the parliament of the federal state of Brandenburg.

Still dissatisfied with the building of the Schloss, Frederick II ordered another palace in Potsdam. The plans came from the King who had previously planned buildings and parklands together with Knobelsdorff. The building period for the single-storey building placed on a slope, the Schloss Sanssouci (1745-1747)—called by the King "My little cottage in the vineyard"—was so short that by 1747 it was ready for occupation.

Johann Conrad Schlaun (1695-1773) created the moated castle of Nordkirchen (1703-1734) and Schloss Munster (1767-1787), regarded as his magnum opus. His signature can be found on a whole series of churches and chapels, monasteries and castles in western Germany. In the small town of Bedburg-Hau, close to the Dutch border,

◀ **Johann Balthasar Neumann,**
Basilica of the Fourteen Holy Helpers,
also known as the *Vierzehnheiligen, 1743-1772.*
Bad Staffelstein.

lies Moyland castle with its massive, zinc-plated towers. It is particularly noteworthy because in 1740 the Prussian King Frederick the Great and Voltaire met there for the first time.

Near Cologne, in Brühl on the Rhine, stands Schloss Augustusburg, named after the Cologne Prince Elector and Archbishop Clemens August who at the same time was also Duke of Westphalia and Bishop of Münster and Paderborn, and the Jadgschloss (hunting lodge) Falkenlust. Under the leadership of Schlaun, work began in 1725 on the planning and building of the three-winged castle. This castle occupies an outstanding position amongst the numerous Rococo buildings in the Rheinland.

Similar to this structure, the small hunting lodge Falkenlust was built in the park by François de Cuvilliés the Elder to serve as a pleasure palace set apart from official duties. The building was modelled after Amalienburg in Munich and Schlosspark Nymphenburg. However, Falkenlust was not intended for the hunting of pheasants but for hunting with falcons, which could be followed from the viewing platform on the roof which served either of the two castles. The castle has a remarkable staircase and ceiling decoration. Both castles are served by large gardens, initially Baroque in style but in the 19th century redesigned as an English landscape park.

Duke Eberhard Ludwig of Württemberg loved to display his absolute power; he visited the château of Versailles and the French court and was incredibly impressed. He utilised these examples and the principles of absolutism as the basis for his own plans and built himself and his long-term mistress one of the largest castles on German soil: the Ludwigsburg Palace, located north of Stuttgart.

The first building to be planned was one of the customary three-wing structures around a large ceremonial courtyard. However, because his own living quarters were located in the main building and did not meet the Duke's requirements for official entertaining, the building had to be extended several times. Ludwigsburg castle, with its 452 rooms, also includes a theatre, two churches and a great park.

The view of the city of Mannheim represents the absolute exception for Germany. Only founded in 1606 by Prince Elector Frederick IV, the city is divided into squares designated by letters and numbers instead of street names. Mannheim Palace (1720-1760), built in the 18th century and counts as one of the largest enclosed Baroque buildings in Europe, with the large, functional courtyard, which is nowadays used for public events.

Bruchsal Palace (1721-c. 1745) is located on the Upper Rhine in the little town of Bruchsal. It was constructed in 1721 as a residence for the Prince-Bishops of Speyer and Constance, Damian Hugo von Schonborn, an avid art collector, whose portrait forms part of a ceiling painting. In accordance with his wishes, the château at Versailles was also to serve as a model for this structure. The unusual arrangement consisted of fifty individual detached buildings, which thus formed a complete district of the city and assumed the functions of a seat of government. The Palace and the town of Bruchsal

were almost completely destroyed shortly before the end of the Second World War. Luckily, the structure of the splendid staircase was mostly preserved.

Margrave Karl III Wilhelm von Baden-Durlach commissioned Albert Friedrich von Kesslau to erect Karlsruhe Palace to reinforce his status. Von Kesslau joined with his teacher, the Frenchman Philippe de La Guêpière, at the court of the Margrave. They built the Karlsruhe Palace according to plans by Balthasar Neumann as a two-storey structure with two long lateral wings connecting with the main building. Burned down in the Second World War, the Schloss was rebuilt and today houses the Baden State Museum.

The most important centre in southern Germany was Munich, a royal residence city in which all epochs were represented, from the Middle Ages through the Renaissance to the Late Baroque period. Here the keen builder Prince Elector Max Emanuel the Generous endeavoured to become a small-scale Louis XIV. The influence of his earlier stay in Paris can be seen from the interior decoration and furnishing of the New Schleissheim Schloss (1701-1726), the Badenburg (1718-1722) and the two-storey Pagodenburg (1716-1719) designed by Prince Elector Max Emanuel.

Already at the beginning of the second quarter of the 18th century, the Paris-trained François de

Egid Quirin Asam and **Cosmas Damian Asam,** ▶
Church of St. Johann Nepomuk, also known as the *Asam Church,* 1733-1746.
Munich.

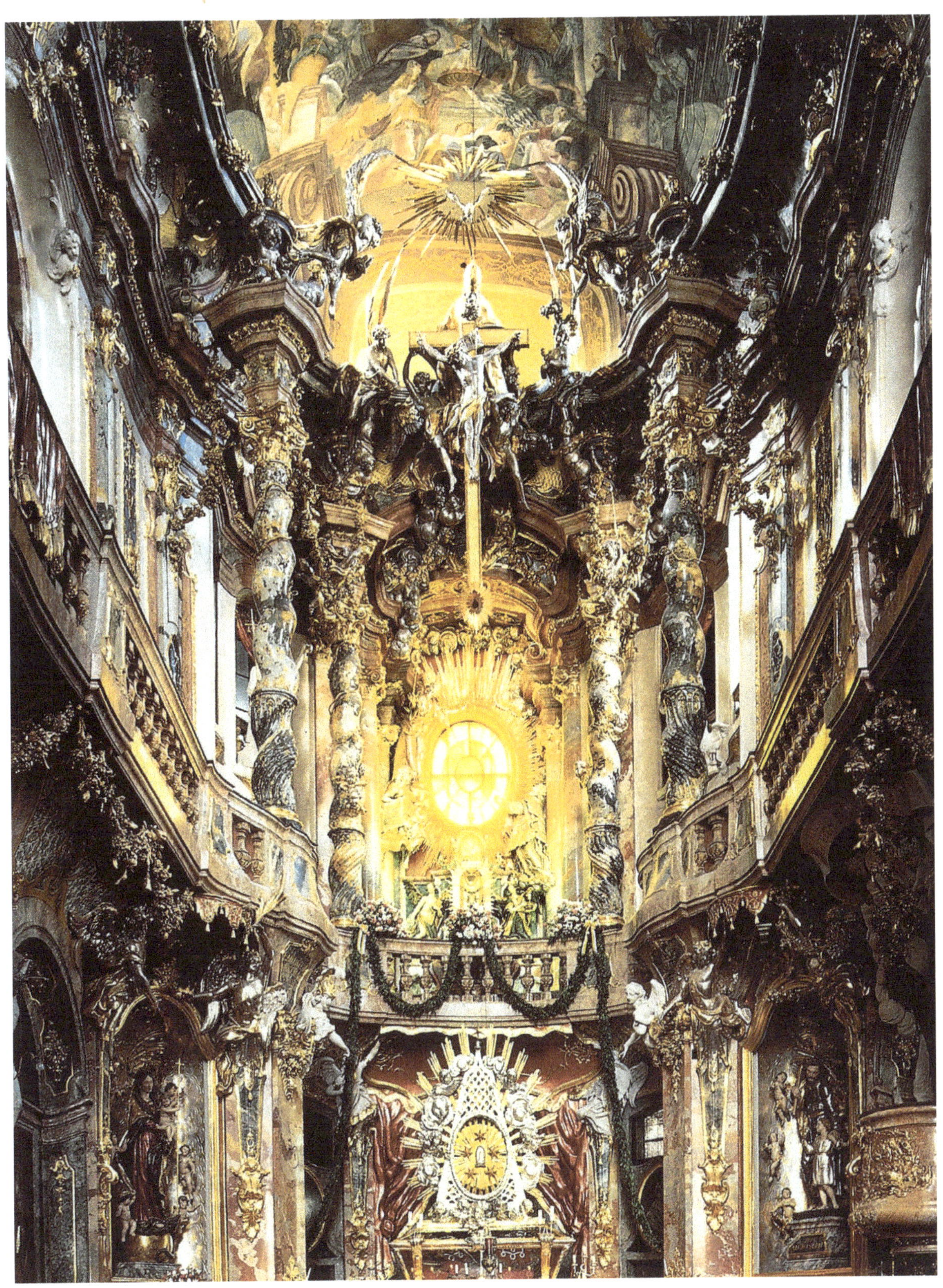

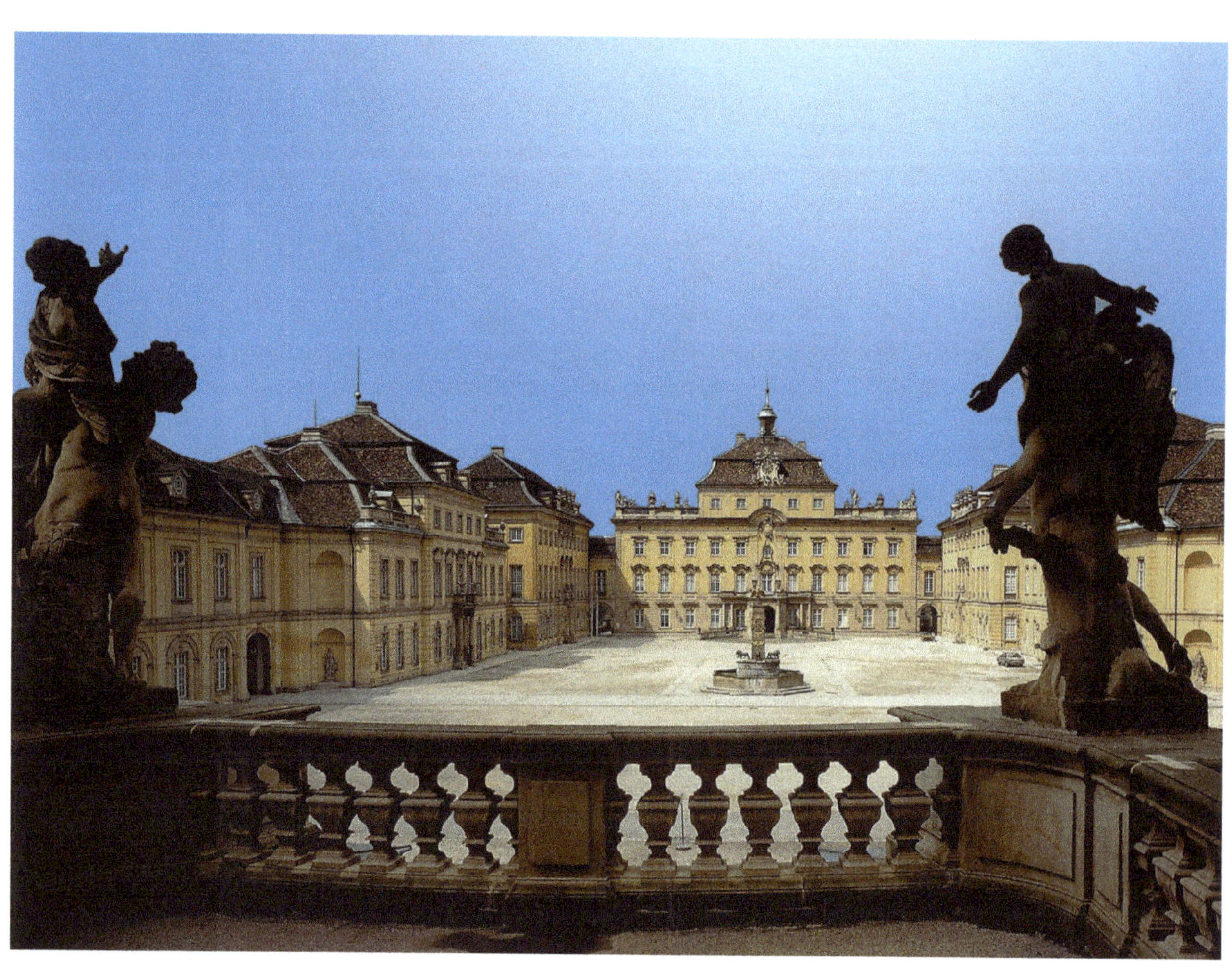

Cuvilliés the Elder travelled to Munich, initially to work there as a court dwarf to the Prince Elector Max Emanuel. However, the Prince soon recognised Cuvilliés's talent and sent him to be trained as an architect first by Joseph Effner, who created the Badenburg and the Pagodenburg, and then to Paris at the Académie Royale d'Architecture. On successful completion of his studies, he was appointed in 1725 as court architect in Munich and from that moment on considerably influenced the building activities in Munich and surrounding areas in the spirit of French Rococo.

One of his first works was a magnificent building, the small single-storey hunting lodge Amalienburg (1734-1739) a present from the Brussels-born Karl Albrecht to his wife Amalie, the daughter of the Austrian Emperor Joseph I (1678-1711). The Amalienburg is one of the earliest and at the same time most beautiful memorials of the Rococo style in Germany.

Through the entrance, one enters directly into a round Hall of Mirrors, whose mirrors reflected the view that comes through the huge windows opposite them. Adjacent are the Hunting Room, the Pheasant Room with its connected kitchen tiled in a thoroughly modern Asiatic style, and the Blue Exhibition Room. The stucco works are particularly interesting, especially *Diana the Goddess of Hunting* enthroned above the

◀ **Johann Friedrich Nette** and **Donato Giuseppe Frisoni**, *Schloss Ludwigsburg*, 1704-1733. Ludwigsburg.

entrance by Johann Baptist Zimmermann, a kindred spirit of Cuvilliés.

In Munich, Cuvilliés the Elder also built the three-storey Holnstein Palace (1733-1737), for which Prince Elector Karl Albrecht had awarded him the commission. Whether Karl Albrecht, like Duke Eberhard Ludwig von Württemberg, intended to accommodate his mistress here or merely his son is a matter of some dispute. Another of Cuvilliés the Elder's important buildings in Munich was the part of the former Munich Royal residence, the Cuvilliés Theatre; it was restored between 2005 and 2008 as one of the most beautiful Rococo theatres.

Balthasar Neumann (1687-1753) constructed an important castle and one of the most significant in Europe, the Residenzschloss Würzburg. Also working with Neumann were the Mainz master builder Maximilian von Welsch, the Genoa-born Viennese architect, one of the greatest of his generation, Lucas von Hildebrandt and, to complete the international character of the project, the two Parisian architects Robert de Cotte and Germain Boffrand, who provided the design for the façade. It is a sure sign of his genius that Neumann succeeded in assembling all these diverse characters despite their independent wishes into a unified entity.

Responsible for laying the foundation stone was Johann Philipp von Schönborn (1673-1724), elected Prince Bishop in 1719, one of the eighteen brothers of Hugo Damian von Schönborn. After his election, widely travelled but deeply unloved by the population, the Prince Bishop decided to build himself a splendid residence, but long before its completion he died of unexplained causes – suppositions range from poisoning to circulatory collapse. His older brother Friedrich Carl von Schönborn oversaw the building process and had it finished.

This residence with its 300 rooms was a compromise between a three wing and a multi-courtyard arrangement. The oversized staircase, as far as the first landing, contains a straight stairway which then splits into two parallel flights of stairs. Giovanni Battista Tiepolo, between 1750 and 1753, created here the largest continuous ceiling fresco in the world. It was restored in 2006, covering approximately 670 square metres. It was the most perfect work of artistic interior decoration of the Rococo period."

A noteworthy exception from the church buildings and onion towers is the Karlskirche (1716-1737) built in Vienna by **Fischer von Erlach** (1656-1723) who was later ennobled. His style, a mixture of Baroque and French Classicism, produced an oval central structure in a projecting broad façade. Other buildings to be ascribed to this period in Vienna were the most beautiful parts of the Court Chancellery, the Court Library and the Trautson Palace (1710-1712). Here in Vienna, the Italian-trained architect Lukas Hildebrand (1668-1745) also worked successfully. He was responsible for the plans for the Prince Eugene of Savoy Palace, the so-called Belvedere (1696-1697).

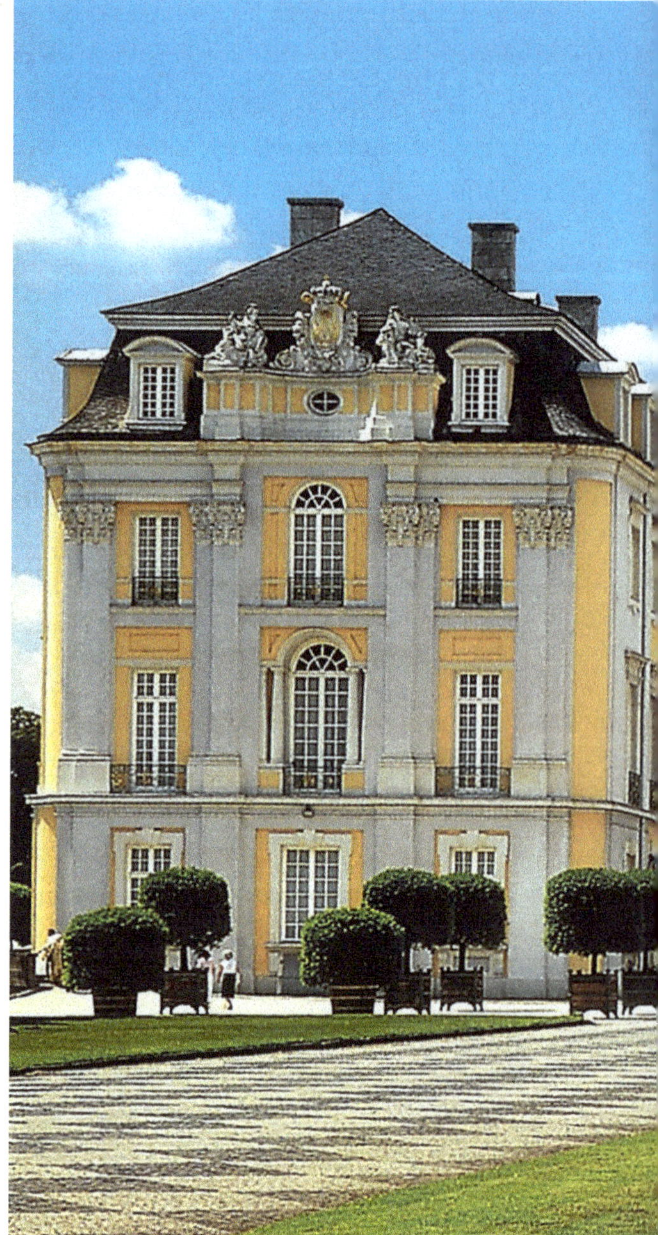

Johann Conrad Schlaun and **François de Cuvilliés,** ▶
Schloss Augustusburg, 1725-1768.
Brühl.

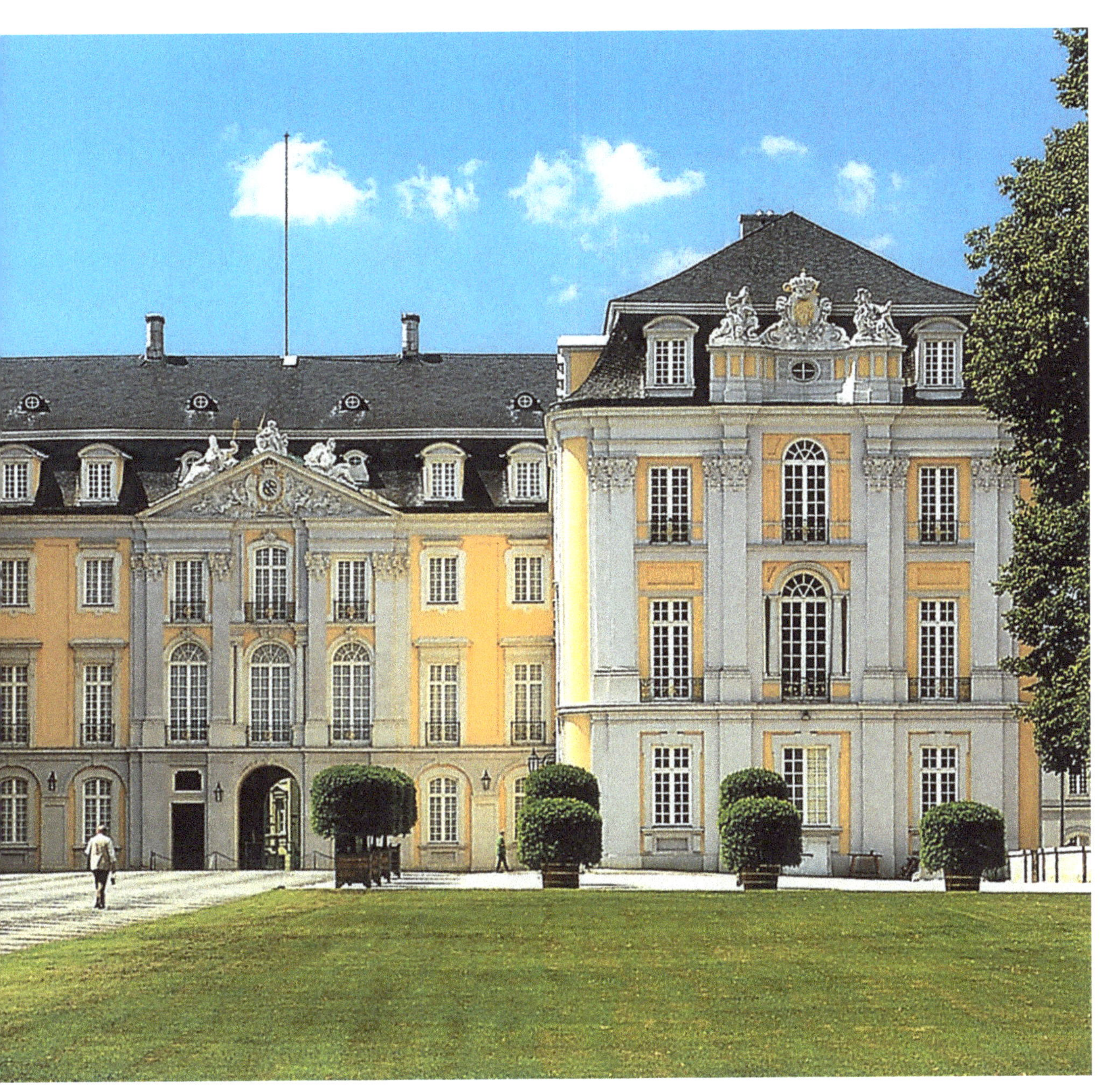

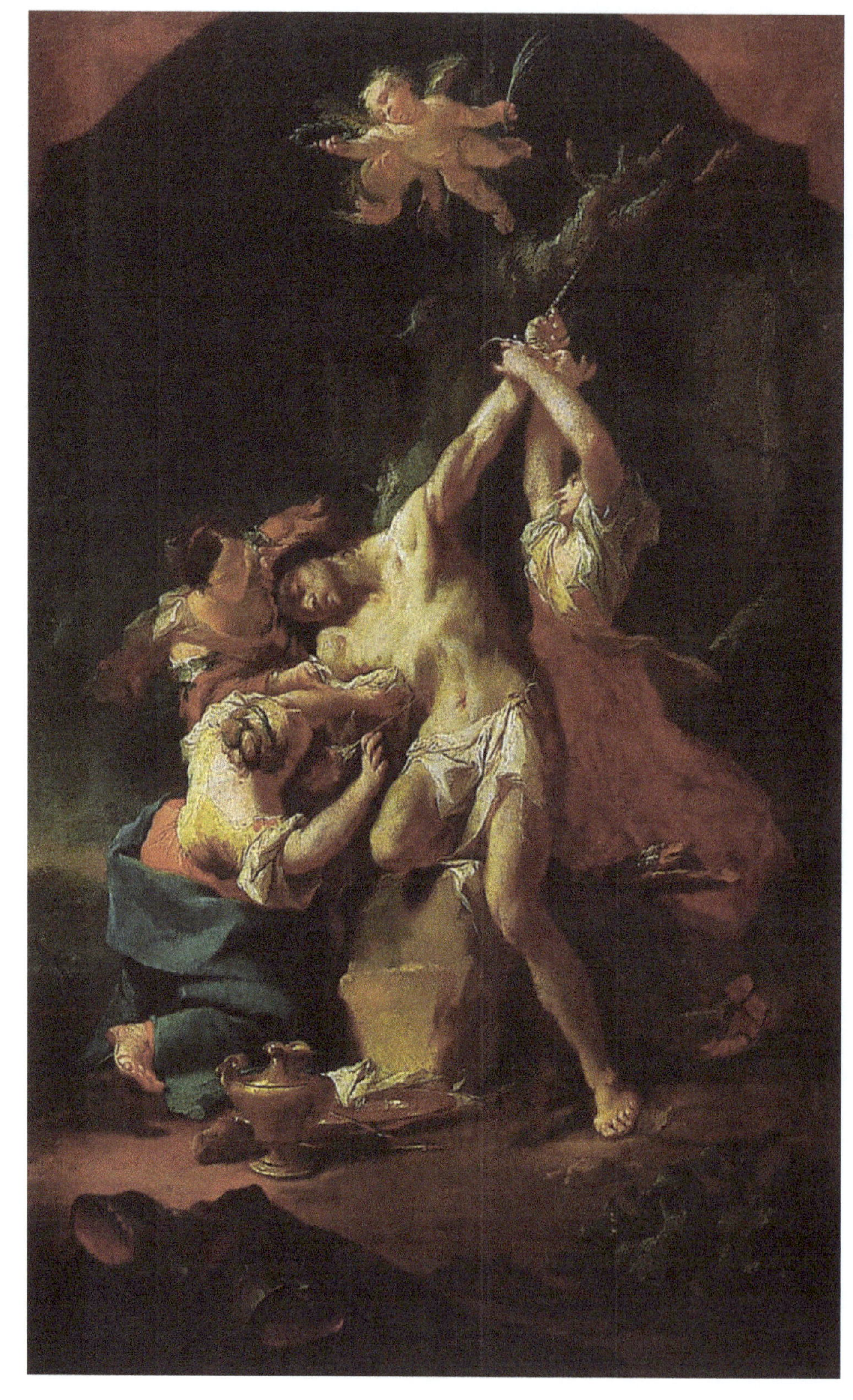

Painting

Rococo painting, as it is known from the work of Boucher, Watteau and others from France, existed neither in Germany nor in other European States. Since the painting of the 18th century possessed an independent meaning, it was based extensively on the traditions of the Baroque period. Most painters of this era had a predominantly regional significance; others were talented technicians, and imitated the older Dutch masters and occasionally in this way achieved a degree of fame in Europe.

Balthasar Denner (1685-1749) painted almost exclusively half-length, head-and-shoulder pictures but with such painstaking treatment of the faces that every little hair, every wrinkle, every little crease in the skin was reproduced with a precision that surpasses microscopic examination. At the same time he demonstrated great respect for age, so that the subjects of his paintings could only feel flattered by such reproductions of nature, for example in the

◀ **Paul Troger**,
St. Sebastian and the Women, c. 1746.
Oil on canvas, 60 x 37 cm.
Belvedere, Vienna.

Portrait of an Old Lady (1720-1745). Balthasar Denner became so popular because of his style of painting that he was summoned to paint portraits in London, Copenhagen and other European capital cities. Even if he did not place all that much emphasis on profound characterisation, he was nevertheless part of the German painters of the 18th century who challenged the French and Italian styles of painting.

Daniel Niklaus Chodowiecki (1726-1801), painter, etcher and drawer from Danzig (Gdansk) was the most fertile of the realists. In 1743 he settled down in Berlin. He was the most objective painter of customs and manners of his age. When he drew, etched or engraved, his guiding principle was always the precise reproduction of reality. Only in his oil paintings did he yield to the prevailing trends in art. His painting of the customs and manners of Berlin society are a feeble echo of Watteau's art and his painted portraits; especially Chodowiecki's miniatures are under French influence. On the other hand, Chodowiecki's engravings and drawings constitute a unique treasure, without which we would have a very incomplete picture of life in the age of King Frederick II the Great.

Pictures from contemporary history, such as his *Delivery Room* (c. 1770), were just as popular as his numerous engravings and etchings for the almanacs. Chodowiecki was celebrated at the time with justification as the first "Illustrator of the Classics," and he proved in his brilliant and lively sketches just how painstakingly accurate and conscientious he was in the work of reproduction. This was illustrated marvellously in his painting *Chodowiecki Paints his Mother*. In this respect Chodowiecki was the forerunner of the great realists of the 19th century.

Johann Christian Thomas Wink (1738-1797 was another from this series was a late Rococo painter who was appointed Court Painter in Munich, and who painted not only many churches but in *Schleissheim* castle he also painted the dining room.

Matthäus Günther (1705-1788), was his teacher was who worked mainly in Bavaria as Director of the Academy of Art in Augsburg, and as a painter of frescoes – approximately 70 frescoes are attributed to him. Wink and Günther, were amongst the most important Rococo painters in Germany.

Anton Raphael Mengs (1728-1779) Raphael Mengs, the son of Ismael Mengs, was an artist in the service of the Saxons. Naturally, Anton Raphael received his first instruction from his father, who taught him, as rumours of the time would have it, more with the whip than the paintbrush. He painted the almost life-sized portraits of King Augustus III (1745), the Queen and the famous singer Regina Mingotti, who at the

time was in the service of the King of Poland. He had a large number of commissions, and painted frescoes in the church of Sant'Eusebio and the chapel of San Caserta, as well as portraits of all his contemporaries. The Spanish King summoned him to his court in Madrid, where he was soon painting the palace with Tiepolo.

The leading painters include **Franz Anton Maulbertsch** (1724-1796), who Oskar Kokoschka claimed as one of his influences. After Maulbertsch had finished the ceiling paintings in the Banquet Hall of Kirchstetten castle, he created the cupola fresco in the Viennese church Maria Treu (1752). He was also responsible for *The Apostle Philippus Baptises a Eunuch* (c. 1750) and the *Victory of St. Jacobus of Compostela* (1762-1764).

Anton von Maron, ▶
Portrait of a Woman (detail).
Oil on canvas, 94.4 x 73.7 cm.
The State Hermitage Museum, St. Petersburg.

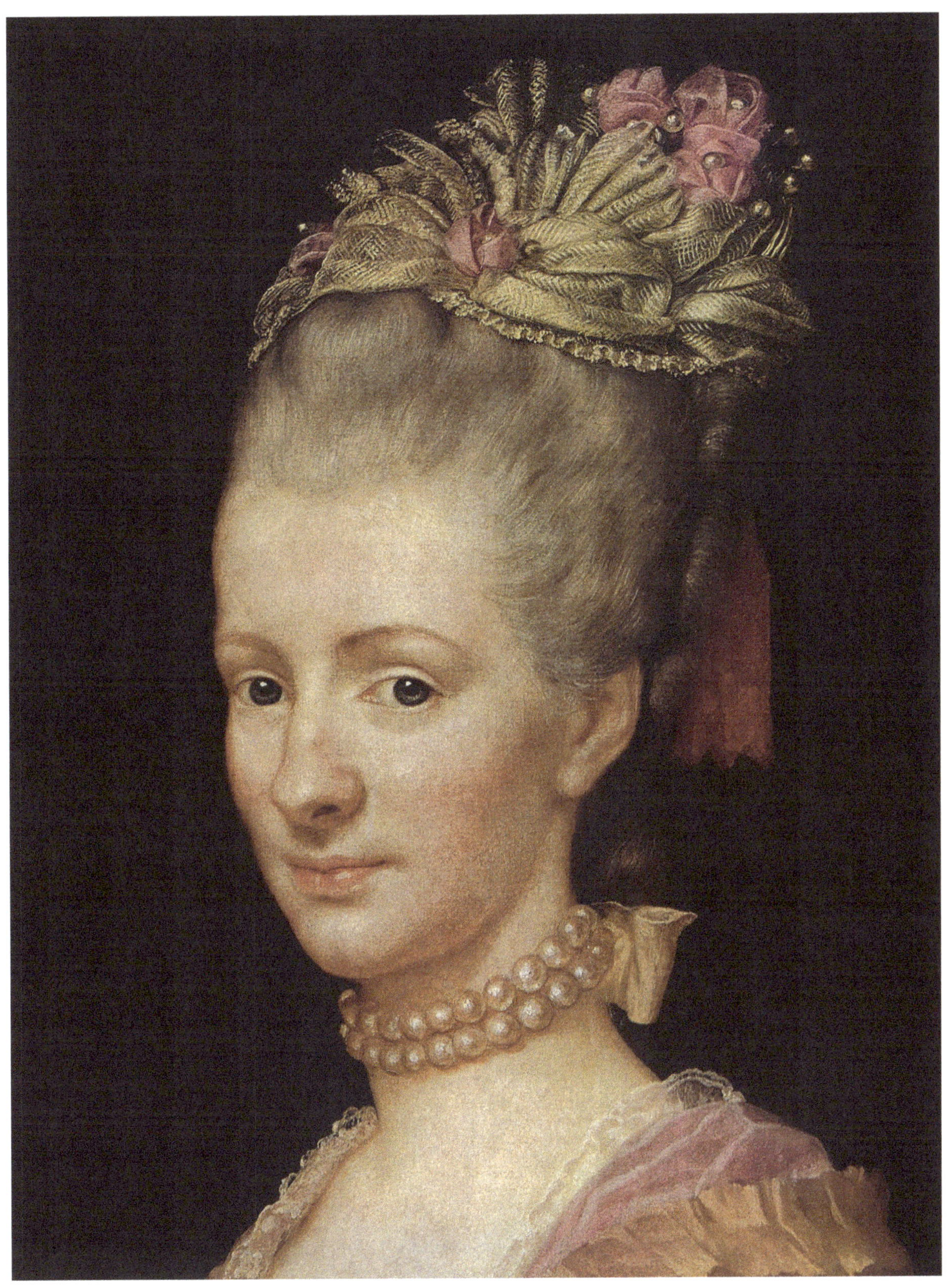

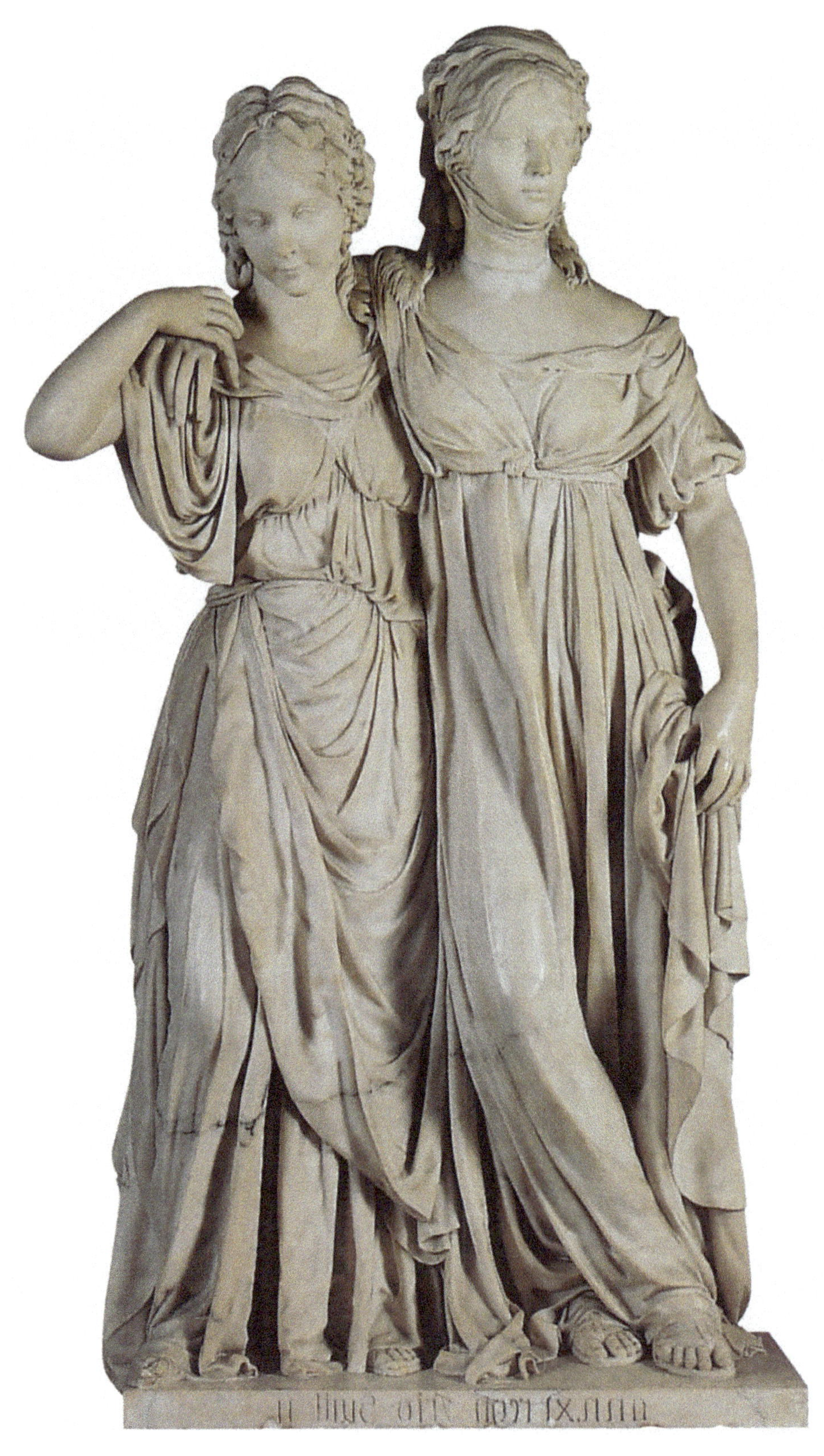

Sculpture

France held a leading position in the fine arts of the 18th century. With the death of the Sun King and the end of absolutism, a clear change in the taste of French patrons could be distinguished, as they began to demand a less grandiose style. It was also the birth of Rococo for sculpture, a light, playful variation on the Baroque style, ideally suited to interior decoration with the new feeling for elaborate asymmetries of flowers, fruits, garlands and rockery, which have a finer, less luxuriant effect than the elements of the Baroque style.

A kind of epicentre for art, which Paris was for France, was lacking in Germany where, particularly at this time, unfavourable general conditions prevailed. German sculpture, which flourished so joyously at the beginning of the 16th century, was by the end of the same century in a state of neglect. The Germans were not able to adapt so quickly to the changed demands which were made of art. Accustomed to giving in their works the expression of profound sensitivity or a certain religious atmosphere, it was difficult for them to find their way into this secularised art form which aimed at ostentation and outward appearances.

Johann Gottfried Schadow (1764-1850), the Prussian sculptor, created the Mausoleum (1790) of Alexander von der Mark, who died as a child. In the Dorotheenkirche in Berlin, an allegorical composition incorporating the spirit of the Rococo age revealed his own natural emotions. Alexander was an illegitimate son of the Frederick William II and his mistress the Countess Wilhelmine von Lichtenau.

Later Schadow veered more towards neoclassicism and created statues of Frederick the Great in Stettin, General von Blücher in Rostock, and of Martin Luther (1483-1546) in Wittenberg. His work also included religious monuments and memorials. Schadow's *Quadriga* on top of the Brandenburg Gate and the allegorical frieze on the façade of the Royal Mint in Berlin were amongst the most beautiful studies modelled after classical art. He wrote a whole series of essays, about such subjects as the national physiognomy and similar themes.

◄ **Johann Gottfried Schadow**,
*The Crown Princesses Louise and
Friederike of Prussia*, 1796-1797.
Marble, 95 x 172 x 59 cm. Alte Nationalgalerie, Berlin.

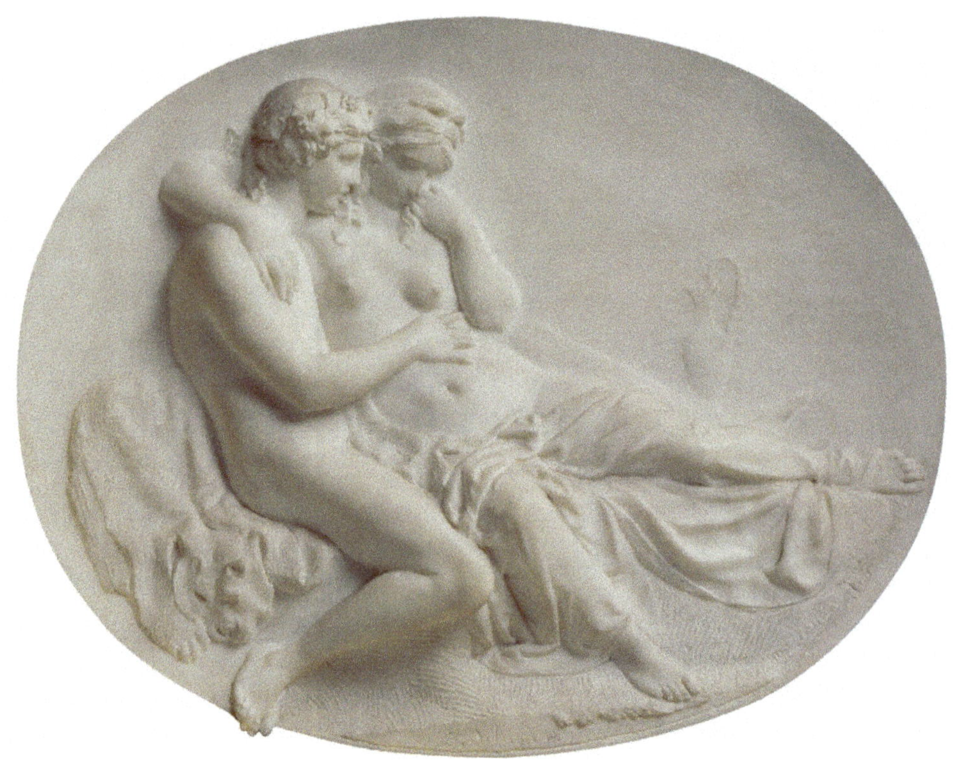

Franz Xavier Messerschmidt (1736-1783) was another outstanding artist of the late Baroque and Early Classical periods. What distinguishes him from numerous other talented south German sculptors around the middle to the end of the 18th century is probably to do with his mental illness which started in the 1770s. Several of his self-portraits from this time came across almost as caricatures. Appointed by Empress Maria Theresia to be her Court Sculptor, he created magnificent, larger-than-life statues of her and her husband Franz I of Lorraine, which may be regarded as typical examples of Messerschmidt's late Baroque style

Georg Rafael Donner (1693-1741 Georg Rafael Donner came from the Viennese school of sculpture. His most important work was the Donner Fountain (1739) on the New Market with the figures placed on the edge of the basin representing the four most important rivers in the Archdukedom. In the centre of the fountain sits the enthroned *Providentia,* which was an allegorical symbol of the city's water supply. Similarly the wall fountain in the Old Town Hall with the *Liberation of Andromeda* (1739), the Sacristy Fountain in St. Stephan's Church (1741) and the altar reliefs in a chapel in St. Martin's Church in Bratislava illustrate this idea.

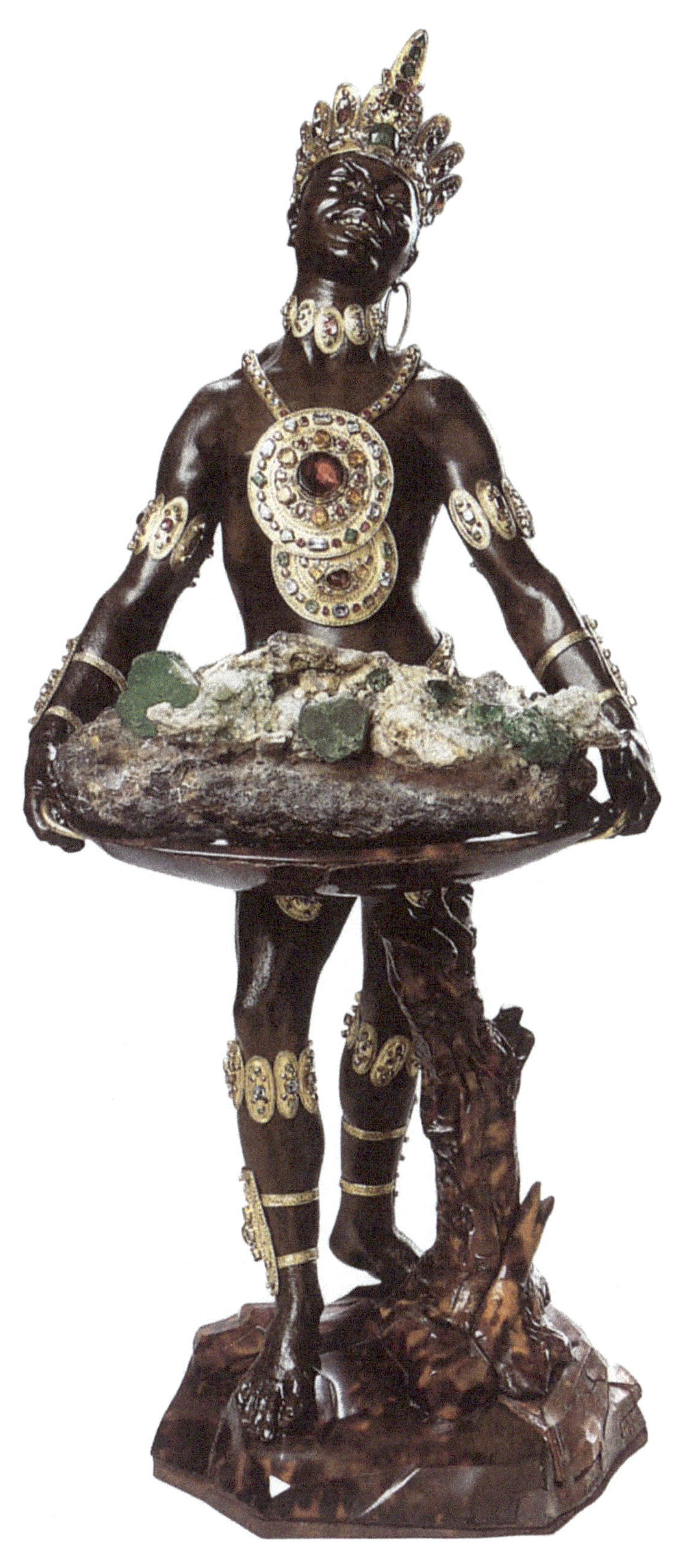

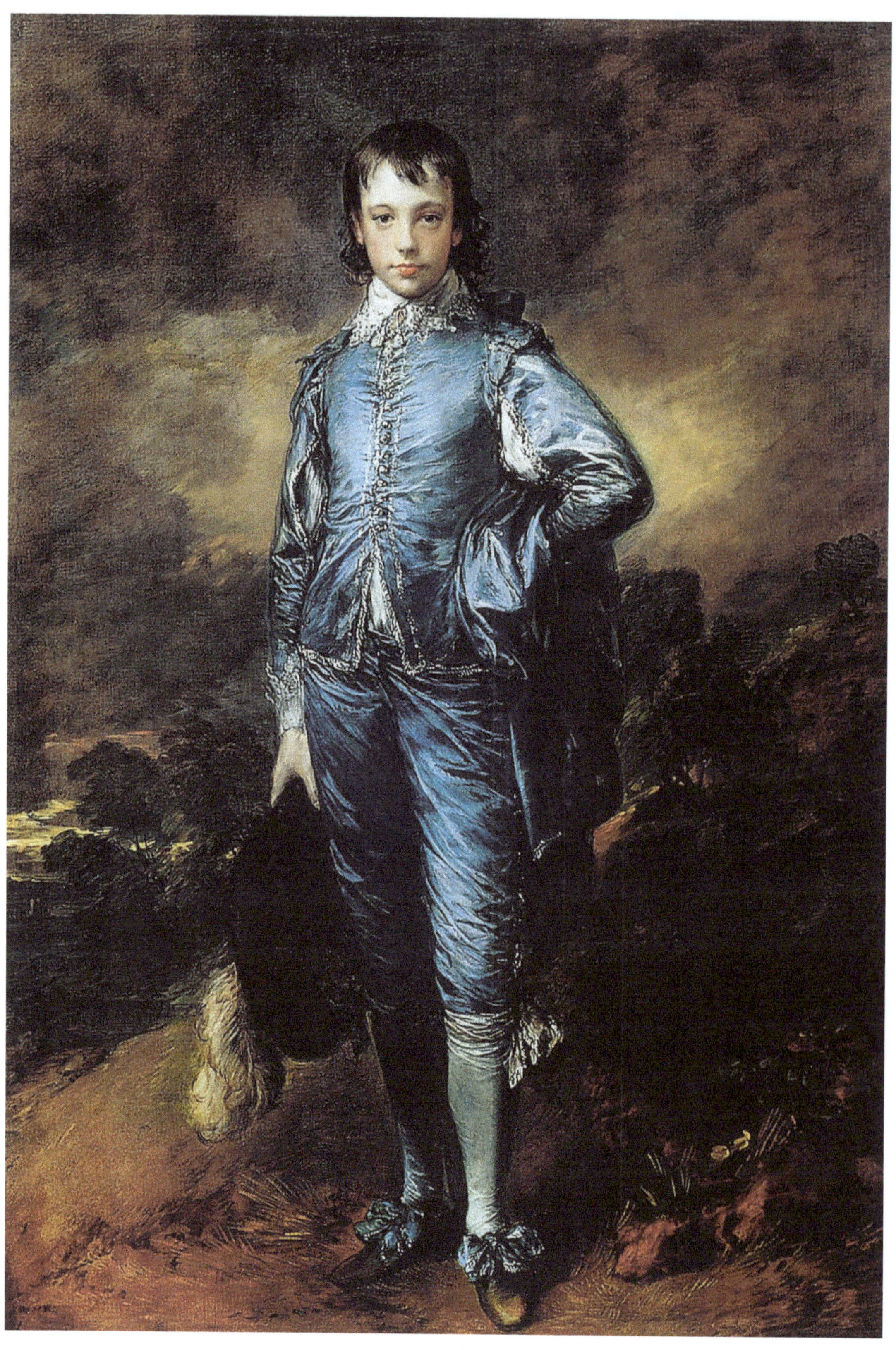

THE 18TH CENTURY IN ENGLAND

Despite the changes evident within other countries, England maintained its isolated position in the history of art, and refused entry to the Roman Catholic Baroque spirit. Even prouder, however, was architecture, which was still strictly dependent on Andrea Palladio ((1508-1580). It was not until well into the 18th century that England possessed its own style of art and architecture. It was primarily the Dutch, but also Germans and Italians who traditionally competed to meet the demand for works of fine art.

Christopher Wren (1632-1723) was one of England's great architects, who until 1667 held a professorial chair in astronomy, but then turned to architecture and from 1669 to 1718 was Royal Court Architect. He began the building of St. Paul's Cathedral in 1675, and it would be the most significant architectural monument in England since the Golden Age of Queen Elizabeth I. Wren started the planning preparations for this building in France. Just like the French at this time, he strove to combine classical discipline with the monumental luxury of Baroque, and he clearly succeeded admirably with this cathedral.

Since the completion of the cathedral, this trend of the English Baroque was also called the Queen Anne style after Queen Anne, the successor to William III. After the Great Fire of London (1666) Wren was given an extensive programme of building to complete, including 51 churches of which 15 are still standing,

Although the Gothic style, rooted deep in the English psyche, occasionally offered resistance to the dominance of classicism, the latter still prevailed throughout the 18th century. Primarily responsible for this were three architects. First, **William Kent** (1685-1748), who was trained in the Roman school and founded the "English landscape style", exerted a major influence on the tastes of the age. Second, the builder of Somerset House, **William Chambers** (1723-1796), placed at the disposal of English architecture and landscape gardening the knowledge he had acquired in extensive travels to the outer reaches of China and the Far East. The third was **George Dance the Younger** (1741-1825), who in addition to several other great buildings in

◀ **Thomas Gainsborough,**
Blue Boy, 1770.
Oil on canvas, 123.8 x 179.4 cm.
The Huntington Library, San Marino.

London not only built Newgate Prison (1769-1778) and the Council Chamber of the Guildhall (1777), but was also responsible for the planning of the Mansion House (1739-1752).

Towards the end of this century, when in France and Germany a renewal of classical antiquity was pursued in architecture, England Romanticism triumphed over Neoclassicism. The national Gothic style remained a determining factor well into the 19th century.

Painting

William Hogarth (1697-1764) was the first painter and engraver who, after an apprenticeship to a silver engraver, looked for his subjects in English folk culture. With pictures duplicated by engravings, of which *The Rake's Progress* (1732-1735) was the finest, Hogarth achieved even greater fame than with his single sheets, which also target political events and frequently direct fierce criticism at those in power. Hogarth, however, was not satisfied with this fame alone. He had the ambition to want to paint historical and religious pictures and this made his fellow citizens and succeeding generations burst out laughing. He did not fare any better when he tried to present himself as his nation's teacher of aesthetics. He gave his opinions about art and the nature of beauty in his book *Analysis of Beauty*.

Hogarth created his most mature works as a portrait painter, even if in this his inclination towards exaggerated characterisation rarely deserted him. Anyone capable of creating such outstanding works as *The Shrimp Girl* or the *Portrait of David Garrick and His Wife* undoubtedly deserves to rank with the great painters.

Joshua Reynolds (1723-1792) as a portrait painter was the second of the great English masters of the 18th century. He established himself, although he too strove more for the laurels of the historical painter. But neither in the strength of his national character nor in the originality of his genius can he be compared with Hogarth. The searching reflection was for Reynolds stronger than his natural temperament and thus it was only after a stay in Italy (1749-1752), where he studied all the great masters, that he truly found his way.

Of the 2000 pictures which he was said to have painted, over half were portraits which achieved their effect particularly through their colouristic charm and through the pleasing nature of the art, not through power or depth of characterisation. To many of his portraits he gave allegorical or mythological titles, such as the picture of children that found fame as *The Age of Innocence*. Just how well Reynolds was able to hone in on the tastes of his contemporaries was shown by the demand for his historical and mythological pictures. A small *Hercules with the Serpent* was greeted with such acclaim that, after selling the original to Tsarina

William Hogarth, ▶
The Shrimp Girl, c. 1740-1745.
Oil on canvas, 63.5 x 52.5 cm.
The National Gallery, London.

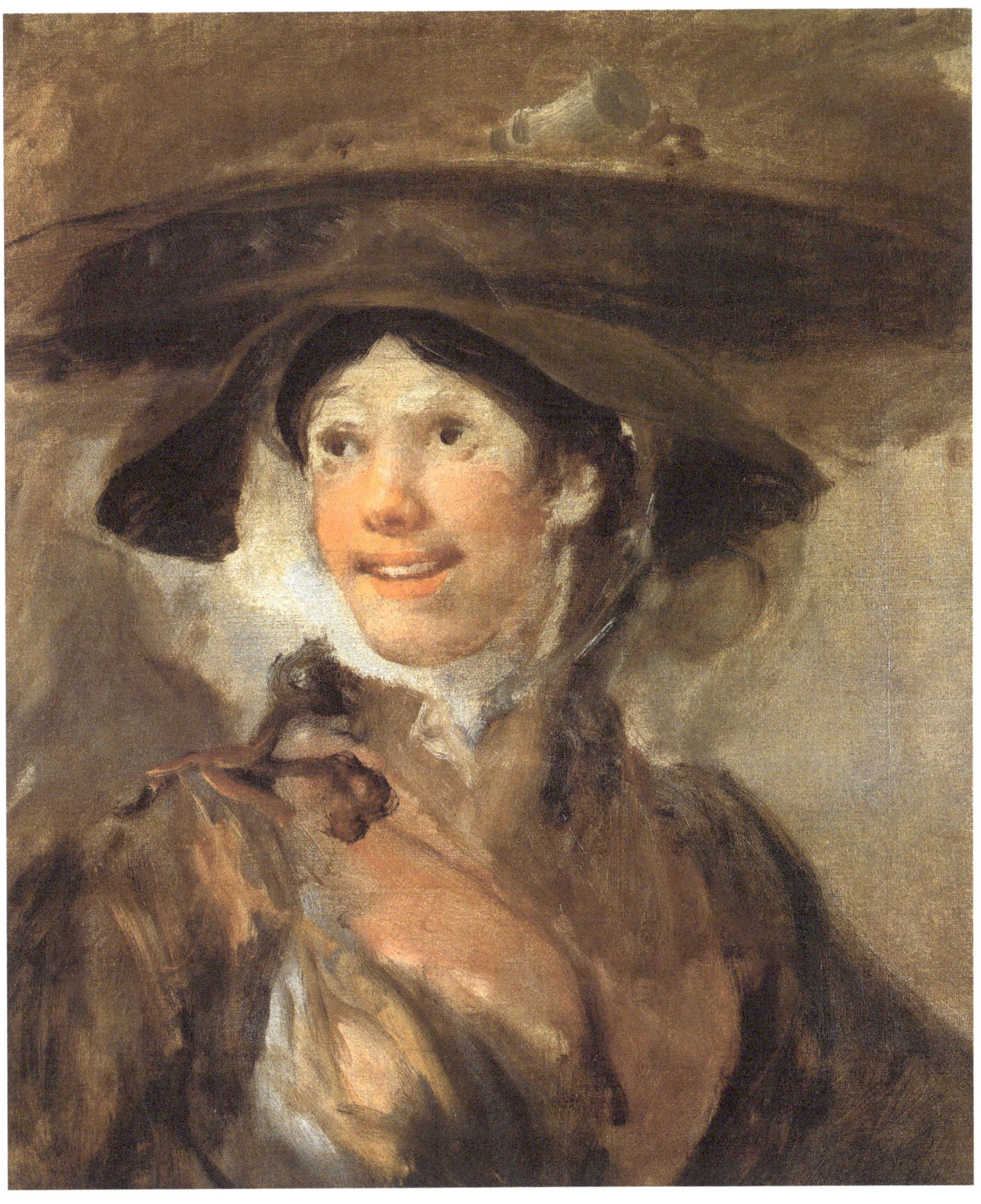

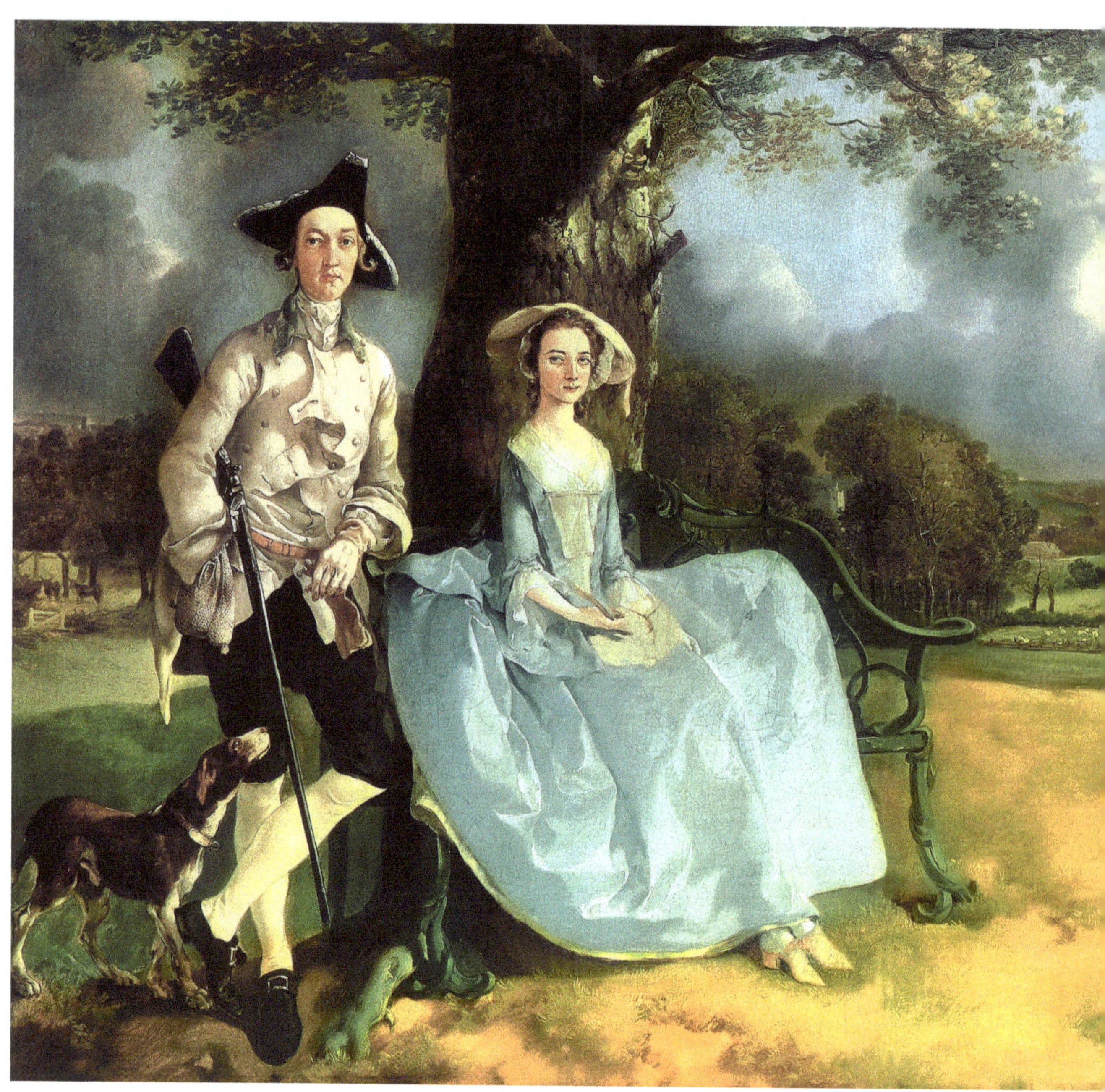

Catherine of Russia, he had to repeat the picture several times.

Thomas Gainsborough (1727-1788) was a much more powerful and elemental nature than Reynolds, and clearly more credible as a portrait painter; he cared little or not at all for the old masters, but rather concerned himself so much more intensively with nature. Here, however, he saw not only the human beings but above all the scenery. For he was equally at home as a landscape painter as he was a portrait painter, so that he can be regarded with confidence as the founder of the English national school of landscape painting, for after all he not only derived his themes from his homeland but he also permeated it with a particularly poetic philosophy, which has remained the basis of the sphere of English landscape painting.

Because of the many years he spent in the most popular spa resort of the age in Bath, Gainsborough had become a preferred painter of the English aristocracy, but he by no means disdained to paint artists, scholars, actors and actresses. The most renowned example of this is the famous *Blue Boy*, the life-sized portrait of Jonathan Buttall, who stands out in his blue clothing from a warm, brown background. Amongst the most famous of Gainsborough's portraits is the portrait of *Mary, Countess Howe.*

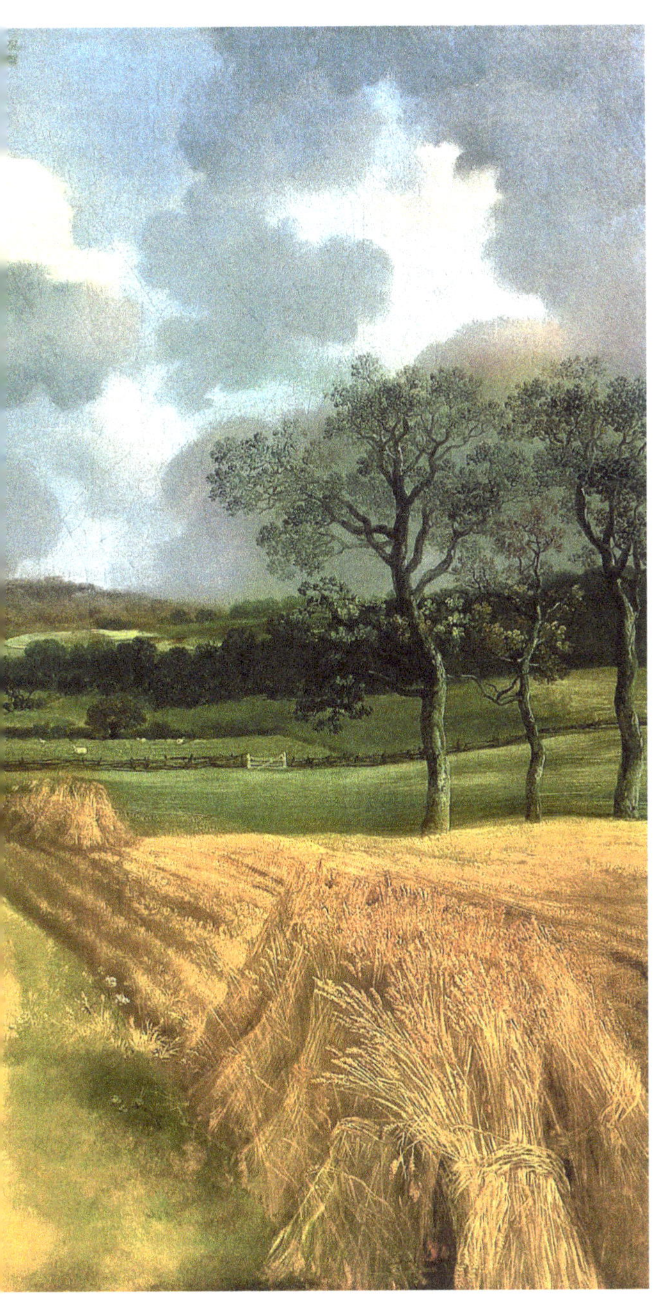

◀ **Thomas Gainsborough,**
Mr. and Mrs. Andrews, c. 1750.
Oil on canvas, 69.8 x 119.4 cm.
The National Gallery, London.

LIST OF ILLUSTRATIONS

ART HISTORY COLLECTION

Abstract Art
Art Deco
Art Nouveau
Baroque
Byzantine Art
Chinese Art
Cubism
Dada
Early Italian Art
Egypt Art
Expressionism
Gothic Art
Greek Art
Impressionism
Indian Art

Naive Art
Neoclassicism
Persian Art
Post-Impressionism
Realism
Renaissance
Pre-Raphaelites
Rococo
Roman Art
Romanesque Art
Romanticism
Surrealism
Symbolism
The Fauves
The Viennese Secession